Trailblazing Trends for AI Self-Driving Cars

Practical Advances in
Artificial Intelligence and Machine Learning

Dr. Lance B. Eliot, MBA, PhD

DEDICATION

To my incredible son, Michael, and my incredible daughter, Lauren.

Forest fortuna adiuvat (from the Latin; good fortune favors the brave).

CONTENTS

Lance B. Eliot

ACKNOWLEDGMENTS

I have been the beneficiary of advice and counsel by many friends, colleagues, family, investors, and many others. I want to thank everyone that has aided me throughout my career. I write from the heart and the head, having experienced first-hand what it means to have others around you that support you during the good times and the tough times.

To Warren Bennis, one of my doctoral advisors and ultimately a colleague, I offer my deepest thanks and appreciation, especially for his calm and insightful wisdom and support.

To Mark Stevens and his generous efforts toward funding and supporting the USC Stevens Center for Innovation.

To Lloyd Greif and the USC Lloyd Greif Center for Entrepreneurial Studies for their ongoing encouragement of founders and entrepreneurs.

To Peter Drucker, William Wang, Aaron Levie, Peter Kim, Jon Kraft, Cindy Crawford, Jenny Ming, Steve Milligan, Chis Underwood, Frank Gehry, Buzz Aldrin, Steve Forbes, Bill Thompson, Dave Dillon, Alan Fuerstman, Larry Ellison, Jim Sinegal, John Sperling, Mark Stevenson, Anand Nallathambi, Thomas Barrack, Jr., and many other innovators and leaders that I have met and gained mightily from doing so.

Thanks to Ed Trainor, Kevin Anderson, James Hickey, Wendell Jones, Ken Harris, DuWayne Peterson, Mike Brown, Jim Thornton, Abhi Beniwal, Al Biland, John Nomura, Eliot Weinman, John Desmond, and many others for their unwavering support during my career.

And most of all thanks as always to Michael and Lauren, for their ongoing support and for having seen me writing and heard much of this material during the many months involved in writing it. To their patience and willingness to listen.

INTRODUCTION

This is a book that provides the newest innovations and the latest Artificial Intelligence (AI) advances about the emerging nature of AI-based autonomous self-driving driverless cars. Via recent advances in Artificial Intelligence (AI) and Machine Learning (ML), we are nearing the day when vehicles can control themselves and will not require and nor rely upon human intervention to perform their driving tasks (or, that <u>allow</u> for human intervention, but only *require* human intervention in very limited ways).

Similar to my other related books, which I describe in a moment and list the chapters in the Appendix A of this book, I am particularly focused on those advances that pertain to self-driving cars. The phrase "autonomous vehicles" is often used to refer to any kind of vehicle, whether it is ground-based or in the air or sea, and whether it is a cargo hauling trailer truck or a conventional passenger car. Though the aspects described in this book are certainly applicable to all kinds of autonomous vehicles, I am focused more so here on cars.

Indeed, I am especially known for my role in aiding the advancement of self-driving cars, serving currently as the Executive Director of the Cybernetic Self-Driving Cars Institute.. In addition to writing software, designing and developing systems and software for self-driving cars, I also speak and write quite a bit about the topic. This book is a collection of some of my more advanced essays. For those of you that might have seen my essays posted elsewhere, I have updated them and integrated them into this book as one handy cohesive package.

You might be interested in companion books that I have written that provide additional key innovations and fundamentals about self-driving cars. Those books are entitled **"Introduction to Driverless Self-Driving Cars," "Advances in AI and Autonomous Vehicles: Cybernetic Self-Driving Cars," "Self-Driving Cars: "The Mother of All AI Projects," "Innovation and Thought Leadership on Self-Driving Driverless Cars," "New Advances in AI Autonomous Driverless Self-Driving Cars,"** and **"Autonomous Vehicle Driverless Self-Driving Cars and**

Artificial Intelligence," "Transformative Artificial Intelligence Driverless Self-Driving Cars," "Disruptive Artificial Intelligence and Driverless Self-Driving Cars, and "State-of-the-Art AI Driverless Self-Driving Cars," and "Top Trends in AI Self-Driving Cars," and "AI Innovations and Self-Driving Cars," "Crucial Advances for AI Driverless Cars," "Sociotechnical Insights and AI Driverless Cars," "Pioneering Advances for AI Driverless Cars" and "Leading Edge Trends for AI Driverless Cars," "The Cutting Edge of AI Autonomous Cars" and "The Next Wave of AI Self-Driving Cars" and "Revolutionary Innovations of AI Self-Driving Cars," and "AI Self-Driving Cars Breakthroughs," and "Trailblazing Trends for AI Self-Driving Cars" (they are all available via Amazon). See Appendix A of this herein book to see a listing of the chapters covered in those three books.

For the introduction here to this book, I am going to borrow my introduction from those companion books, since it does a good job of laying out the landscape of self-driving cars and my overall viewpoints on the topic. The remainder of the book is all new material that does not appear in the companion books.

INTRODUCTION TO SELF-DRIVING CARS

This is a book about self-driving cars. Someday in the future, we'll all have self-driving cars and this book will perhaps seem antiquated, but right now, we are at the forefront of the self-driving car wave. Daily news bombards us with flashes of new announcements by one car maker or another and leaves the impression that within the next few weeks or maybe months that the self-driving car will be here. A casual non-technical reader would assume from these news flashes that in fact we must be on the cusp of a true self-driving car.

Here's a real news flash: We are still quite a distance from having a true self-driving car. It is years to go before we get there.

Why is that? Because a true self-driving car is akin to a moonshot. In the same manner that getting us to the moon was an incredible feat, likewise can it be said for achieving a true self-driving car. Anybody that suggests or even brashly states that the true self-driving car is nearly here should be viewed with great skepticism. Indeed, you'll see that I often tend to use the word "hogwash" or "crock" when I assess much of the decidedly *fake news* about self-driving cars. Those of us on the inside know that what is often reported to the outside is malarkey. Few of the insiders are willing to say so. I have no such hesitation.

Indeed, I've been writing a popular blog post about self-driving cars and hitting hard on those that try to wave their hands and pretend that we are on the imminent verge of true self-driving cars. For many years, I've been known as the AI Insider. Besides writing about AI, I also develop AI software. I do what I describe. It also gives me insights into what others that are doing AI are really doing versus what it is said they are doing.

Many faithful readers had asked me to pull together my insightful short essays and put them into another book, which you are now holding in your hands.

For those of you that have been reading my essays over the years, this collection not only puts them together into one handy package, I also updated the essays and added new material. For those of you that are new to the topic of self-driving cars and AI, I hope you find these essays approachable and informative. I also tend to have a writing style with a bit of a voice, and so you'll see that I am times have a wry sense of humor and poke at conformity.

As a former professor and founder of an AI research lab, I for many years wrote in the formal language of academic writing. I published in referred journals and served as an editor for several AI journals. This writing here is not of the nature, and I have adopted a different and more informal style for these essays. That being said, I also do mention from time-to-time more rigorous material on AI and encourage you all to dig into those deeper and more formal materials if so interested.

I am also an AI practitioner. This means that I write AI software for a living. Currently, I head-up the Cybernetics Self-Driving Car Institute, where we are developing AI software for self-driving cars. I am excited to also report that my son, also a software engineer, heads-up our Cybernetics Self-Driving Car Lab. What I have helped to start, and for which he is an integral part, ultimately he will carry long into the future after I have retired. My daughter, a marketing whiz, also is integral to our efforts as head of our Marketing group. She too will carry forward the legacy now being formulated.

For those of you that are reading this book and have a penchant for writing code, you might consider taking a look at the open source code available for self-driving cars. This is a handy place to start learning how to develop AI for self-driving cars. There are also many new educational courses spring forth. There is a growing body of those wanting to learn about and develop self-driving cars, and a growing body of colleges, labs, and other avenues by which you can learn about self-driving cars.

This book will provide a foundation of aspects that I think will get you ready for those kinds of more advanced training opportunities. If you've already taken those classes, you'll likely find these essays especially interesting as they offer a perspective that I am betting few other instructors or faculty offered to you. These are challenging essays that ask you to think beyond the conventional about self-driving cars.

THE MOTHER OF ALL AI PROJECTS

In June 2017, Apple CEO Tim Cook came out and finally admitted that Apple has been working on a self-driving car. As you'll see in my essays, Apple was enmeshed in secrecy about their self-driving car efforts. We have only been able to read the tea leaves and guess at what Apple has been up to. The notion of an iCar has been floating for quite a while, and self-driving engineers and researchers have been signing tight-lipped Non-Disclosure Agreements (NDA's) to work on projects at Apple that were as shrouded in mystery as any military invasion plans might be.

Tim Cook said something that many others in the Artificial Intelligence (AI) field have been saying, namely, the creation of a self-driving car has got to be the mother of all AI projects. In other words, it is in fact a tremendous moonshot for AI. If a self-driving car can be crafted and the AI works as we hope, it means that we have made incredible strides with AI and that therefore it opens many other worlds of potential breakthrough accomplishments that AI can solve.

Is this hyperbole? Am I just trying to make AI seem like a miracle worker and so provide self-aggrandizing statements for those of us writing the AI software for self-driving cars? No, it is not hyperbole. Developing a true self-driving car is really, really, really hard to do. Let me take a moment to explain why. As a side note, I realize that the Apple CEO is known for at times uttering hyperbole, and he had previously said for example that the year 2012 was "the mother of all years," and he had said that the release of iOS 10 was "the mother of all releases" – all of which does suggest he likes to use the handy "mother of" expression. But, I assure you, in terms of true self-driving cars, he has hit the nail on the head. For sure.

When you think about a moonshot and how we got to the moon, there are some identifiable characteristics and those same aspects can be applied to creating a true self-driving car. You'll notice that I keep putting the word "true" in front of the self-driving car expression. I do so because as per my essay about the various levels of self-driving cars, there are some self-driving cars that are only somewhat of a self-driving car. The somewhat versions are ones that require a human driver to be ready to intervene. In my view, that's not a true self-driving car. A true self-driving car is one that requires no human driver intervention at all. It is a car that can entirely undertake via automation the driving task without any human driver needed. This is the essence of what is known as a Level 5 self-driving car. We are currently at the Level 2 and Level 3 mark, and not yet at Level 5.

Getting to the moon involved aspects such as having big stretch goals, incremental progress, experimentation, innovation, and so on. Let's review how this applied to the moonshot of the bygone era, and how it applies to the self-driving car moonshot of today.

Big Stretch Goal

Trying to take a human and deliver the human to the moon, and bring them back, safely, was an extremely large stretch goal at the time. No one knew whether it could be done. The technology wasn't available yet. The cost was huge. The determination would need to be fierce. Etc. To reach a Level 5 self-driving car is going to be the same. It is a big stretch goal. We can readily get to the Level 3, and we are able to see the Level 4 just up ahead, but a Level 5 is still an unknown as to if it is doable. It should eventually be doable and in the same way that we thought we'd eventually get to the moon, but when it will occur is a different story.

Incremental Progress

Getting to the moon did not happen overnight in one fell swoop. It took years and years of incremental progress to get there. Likewise for self-driving cars. Google has famously been striving to get to the Level 5, and pretty much been willing to forgo dealing with the intervening levels, but most of the other self-driving car makers are doing the incremental route. Let's get a good Level 2 and a somewhat Level 3 going. Then, let's improve the Level 3 and get a somewhat Level 4 going. Then, let's improve the Level 4 and finally arrive at a Level 5. This seems to be the prevalent way that we are going to achieve the true self-driving car.

Experimentation

You likely know that there were various experiments involved in perfecting the approach and technology to get to the moon. As per making incremental progress, we first tried to see if we could get a rocket to go into space and safety return, then put a monkey in there, then with a human, then we went all the way to the moon but didn't land, and finally we arrived at the mission that actually landed on the moon. Self-driving cars are the same way. We are doing simulations of self-driving cars. We do testing of self-driving cars on private land under controlled situations. We do testing of self-driving cars on public roadways, often having to meet regulatory requirements including for example having an engineer or equivalent in the car to take over the controls if needed. And so on. Experiments big and small are needed to figure out what works and what doesn't.

Innovation

There are already some advances in AI that are allowing us to progress toward self-driving cars. We are going to need even more advances. Innovation in all aspects of technology are going to be required to achieve a true self-driving car. By no means do we already have everything in-hand that we need to get there. Expect new inventions and new approaches, new algorithms, etc.

Setbacks

Most of the pundits are avoiding talking about potential setbacks in the progress toward self-driving cars. Getting to the moon involved many setbacks, some of which you never have heard of and were buried at the time so as to not dampen enthusiasm and funding for getting to the moon. A recurring theme in many of my included essays is that there are going to be setbacks as we try to arrive at a true self-driving car. Take a deep breath and be ready. I just hope the setbacks don't completely stop progress. I am sure that it will cause progress to alter in a manner that we've not yet seen in the self-driving car field. I liken the self-driving car of today to the excitement everyone had for Uber when it first got going. Today, we have a different view of Uber and with each passing day there are more regulations to the ride sharing business and more concerns raised. The darling child only stays a darling until finally that child acts up. It will happen the same with self-driving cars.

SELF-DRIVING CARS CHALLENGES

But what exactly makes things so hard to have a true self-driving car, you might be asking. You have seen cruise control for years and years. You've lately seen cars that can do parallel parking. You've seen YouTube videos of Tesla drivers that put their hands out the window as their car zooms along the highway, and seen to therefore be in a self-driving car. Aren't we just needing to put a few more sensors onto a car and then we'll have in-hand a true self-driving car? Nope.

Consider for a moment the nature of the driving task. We don't just let anyone at any age drive a car. Worldwide, most countries won't license a driver until the age of 18, though many do allow a learner's permit at the age of 15 or 16. Some suggest that a younger age would be physically too small to reach the controls of the car. Though this might be the case, we could easily adjust the controls to allow for younger aged and thus smaller stature. It's not their physical size that matters. It's their cognitive development that matters.

To drive a car, you need to be able to reason about the car, what the car can and cannot do. You need to know how to operate the car. You need to know about how other cars on the road drive. You need to know what is allowed in driving such as speed limits and driving within marked lanes. You need to be able to react to situations and be able to avoid getting into accidents. You need to ascertain when to hit your brakes, when to steer clear of a pedestrian, and how to keep from ramming that motorcyclist that just cut you off.

Many of us had taken courses on driving. We studied about driving and took driver training. We had to take a test and pass it to be able to drive. The point being that though most adults take the driving task for granted, and we often "mindlessly" drive our cars, there is a significant amount of cognitive effort that goes into driving a car. After a while, it becomes second nature. You don't especially think about how you drive, you just do it. But, if you watch a novice driver, say a teenager learning to drive, you suddenly realize that there is a lot more complexity to it than we seem to realize.

Furthermore, driving is a very serious task. I recall when my daughter and son first learned to drive. They are both very conscientious people. They wanted to make sure that whatever they did, they did well, and that they did not harm anyone. Every day, when you get into a car, it is probably around 4,000 pounds of hefty metal and plastics (about two tons), and it is a lethal weapon. Think about it. You drive down the street in an object that weighs two tons and with the engine it can accelerate and ram into anything you want to hit. The damage a car can inflict is very scary. Both my children were surprised that they were being given the right to maneuver this monster of a beast that could cause tremendous harm entirely by merely letting go of the steering wheel for a moment or taking your eyes off the road.

In fact, in the United States alone there are about 30,000 deaths per year by auto accidents, which is around 100 per day. Given that there are about 263 million cars in the United States, I am actually more amazed that the number of fatalities is not a lot higher. During my morning commute, I look at all the thousands of cars on the freeway around me, and I think that if all of them decided to go zombie and drive in a crazy maniac way, there would be many people dead. Somehow, incredibly, each day, most people drive relatively safely. To me, that's a miracle right there. Getting millions and millions of people to be safe and sane when behind the wheel of a two ton mobile object, it's a feat that we as a society should admire with pride.

So, hopefully you are in agreement that the driving task requires a great deal of cognition. You don't' need to be especially smart to drive a car, and we've done quite a bit to make car driving viable for even the average dolt. There isn't an IQ test that you need to take to drive a car. If you can read and write, and pass a test, you pretty much can legally drive a car. There are of course some that drive a car and are not legally permitted to do so, plus there are private areas such as farms where drivers are young, but for public roadways in the United States, you can be generally of average intelligence (or less) and be able to legally drive.

This though makes it seem like the cognitive effort must not be much. If the cognitive effort was truly hard, wouldn't we only have Einstein's that could drive a car? We have made sure to keep the driving task as simple as we can, by making the controls easy and relatively standardized, and by having roads that are relatively standardized, and so on. It is as though Disneyland has put their Autopia into the real-world, by us all as a society agreeing that roads will be a certain way, and we'll all abide by the various rules of driving.

A modest cognitive task by a human is still something that stymies AI. You certainly know that AI has been able to beat chess players and be good at other kinds of games. This type of narrow cognition is not what car driving is about. Car driving is much wider. It requires knowledge about the world, which a chess playing AI system does not need to know. The cognitive aspects of driving are on the one hand seemingly simple, but at the same time require layer upon layer of knowledge about cars, people, roads, rules, and a myriad of other "common sense" aspects. We don't have any AI systems today that have that same kind of breadth and depth of awareness and knowledge.

As revealed in my essays, the self-driving car of today is using trickery to do particular tasks. It is all very narrow in operation. Plus, it currently assumes that a human driver is ready to intervene. It is like a child that we have taught to stack blocks, but we are needed to be right there in case the child stacks them too high and they begin to fall over. AI of today is brittle, it is narrow, and it does not approach the cognitive abilities of humans. This is why the true self-driving car is somewhere out in the future.

Another aspect to the driving task is that it is not solely a mind exercise. You do need to use your senses to drive. You use your eyes a vision sensors to see the road ahead. You vision capability is like a streaming video, which your brain needs to continually analyze as you drive. Where is the road? Is there a pedestrian in the way? Is there another car ahead of you? Your senses are relying a flood of info to your brain. Self-driving cars are trying to do the same, by using cameras, radar, ultrasound, and lasers. This is an attempt at mimicking how humans have senses and sensory apparatus.

Thus, the driving task is mental and physical. You use your senses, you use your arms and legs to manipulate the controls of the car, and you use your brain to assess the sensory info and direct your limbs to act upon the controls of the car. This all happens instantly. If you've ever perhaps gotten something in your eye and only had one eye available to drive with, you suddenly realize how dependent upon vision you are. If you have a broken foot with a cast, you suddenly realize how hard it is to control the brake pedal and the accelerator. If you've taken medication and your brain is maybe sluggish, you suddenly realize how much mental strain is required to drive a car.

An AI system that plays chess only needs to be focused on playing chess. The physical aspects aren't important because usually a human moves the chess pieces or the chessboard is shown on an electronic display. Using AI for a more life-and-death task such as analyzing MRI images of patients, this again does not require physical capabilities and instead is done by examining images of bits.

Driving a car is a true life-and-death task. It is a use of AI that can easily and at any moment produce death. For those colleagues of mine that are developing this AI, as am I, we need to keep in mind the somber aspects of this. We are producing software that will have in its virtual hands the lives of the occupants of the car, and the lives of those in other nearby cars, and the lives of nearby pedestrians, etc. Chess is not usually a life-or-death matter.

Driving is all around us. Cars are everywhere. Most of today's AI applications involve only a small number of people. Or, they are behind the scenes and we as humans have other recourse if the AI messes up. AI that is driving a car at 80 miles per hour on a highway had better not mess up. The consequences are grave. Multiply this by the number of cars, if we could put magically self-driving into every car in the USA, we'd have AI running in the 263 million cars. That's a lot of AI spread around. This is AI on a massive scale that we are not doing today and that offers both promise and potential peril.

There are some that want AI for self-driving cars because they envision a world without any car accidents. They envision a world in which there is no car congestion and all cars cooperate with each other. These are wonderful utopian visions.

They are also very misleading. The adoption of self-driving cars is going to be incremental and not overnight. We cannot economically just junk all existing cars. Nor are we going to be able to affordably retrofit existing cars. It is more likely that self-driving cars will be built into new cars and that over many years of gradual replacement of existing cars that we'll see the mix of self-driving cars become substantial in the real-world.

In these essays, I have tried to offer technological insights without being overly technical in my description, and also blended the business, societal, and economic aspects too. Technologists need to consider the non-technological impacts of what they do. Non-technologists should be aware of what is being developed.

We all need to work together to collectively be prepared for the enormous disruption and transformative aspects of true self-driving cars. We all need to be involved in this mother of all AI projects.

WHAT THIS BOOK PROVIDES

What does this book provide to you? It introduces many of the key elements about self-driving cars and does so with an AI based perspective. I weave together technical and non-technical aspects, readily going from being concerned about the cognitive capabilities of the driving task and how the technology is embodying this into self-driving cars, and in the next breath I discuss the societal and economic aspects.

They are all intertwined because that's the way reality is. You cannot separate out the technology per se, and instead must consider it within the milieu of what is being invented and innovated, and do so with a mindset towards the contemporary mores and culture that shape what we are doing and what we hope to do.

WHY THIS BOOK

I wrote this book to try and bring to the public view many aspects about self-driving cars that nobody seems to be discussing.

For business leaders that are either involved in making self-driving cars or that are going to leverage self-driving cars, I hope that this book will enlighten you as to the risks involved and ways in which you should be strategizing about how to deal with those risks.

For entrepreneurs, startups and other businesses that want to enter into the self-driving car market that is emerging, I hope this book sparks your interest in doing so, and provides some sense of what might be prudent to pursue.

For researchers that study self-driving cars, I hope this book spurs your interest in the risks and safety issues of self-driving cars, and also nudges you toward conducting research on those aspects.

For students in computer science or related disciplines, I hope this book will provide you with interesting and new ideas and material, for which you might conduct research or provide some career direction insights for you.

For AI companies and high-tech companies pursuing self-driving cars, this book will hopefully broaden your view beyond just the mere coding and development needed to make self-driving cars.

For all readers, I hope that you will find the material in this book to be stimulating. Some of it will be repetitive of things you already know. But I am pretty sure that you'll also find various eureka moments whereby you'll discover a new technique or approach that you had not earlier thought of. I am also betting that there will be material that forces you to rethink some of your current practices.

I am not saying you will suddenly have an epiphany and change what you are doing. I do think though that you will reconsider or perhaps revisit what you are doing.

For anyone choosing to use this book for teaching purposes, please take a look at my suggestions for doing so, as described in the Appendix. I have found the material handy in courses that I have taught, and likewise other faculty have told me that they have found the material handy, in some cases as extended readings and in other instances as a core part of their course (depending on the nature of the class).

In my writing for this book, I have tried carefully to blend both the practitioner and the academic styles of writing. It is not as dense as is typical academic journal writing, but at the same time offers depth by going into the nuances and trade-offs of various practices.

The word "deep" is in vogue today, meaning getting deeply into a subject or topic, and so is the word "unpack" which means to tease out the underlying aspects of a subject or topic. I have sought to offer material that addresses an issue or topic by going relatively deeply into it and make sure that it is well unpacked.

Finally, in any book about AI, it is difficult to use our everyday words without having some of them be misinterpreted. Specifically, it is easy to anthropomorphize AI. When I say that an AI system "knows" something, I do not want you to construe that the AI system has sentience and "knows" in the same way that humans do. They aren't that way, as yet. I have tried to use quotes around such words from time-to-time to emphasize that the words I am using should not be misinterpreted to ascribe true human intelligence to the AI systems that we know of today. If I used quotes around all such words, the book would be very difficult to read, and so I am doing so judiciously. Please keep that in mind as you read the material, thanks.

COMPANION BOOKS

If you find this material of interest, you might enjoy these too:

1. **"Introduction to Driverless Self-Driving Cars"** by Dr. Lance Eliot

2. **"Innovation and Thought Leadership on Self-Driving Driverless Cars"** by Dr. Lance Eliot

3. **"Advances in AI and Autonomous Vehicles: Cybernetic Self-Driving Cars"** by Dr. Lance Eliot

4. **"Self-Driving Cars: The Mother of All AI Projects"** by Dr. Lance Eliot

5. **"New Advances in AI Autonomous Driverless Self-Driving Cars"** by Dr. Lance Eliot

6. **"Autonomous Vehicle Driverless Self-Driving Cars and Artificial Intelligence"** by Dr. Lance Eliot and Michael B. Eliot

7. **"Transformative Artificial Intelligence Driverless Self-Driving Cars"** by Dr. Lance Eliot

8. **"Disruptive Artificial Intelligence and Driverless Self-Driving Cars"** by Dr. Lance Eliot

9. "State-of-the-Art AI Driverless Self-Driving Cars" by Dr. Lance Eliot

10. **"Top Trends in AI Self-Driving Cars"** by Dr. Lance Eliot

11. **"AI Innovations and Self-Driving Cars"** by Dr. Lance Eliot

12. **"Crucial Advances for AI Driverless Cars"** by Dr. Lance Eliot

13. **"Sociotechnical Insights and AI Driverless Cars"** by Dr. Lance Eliot.

14. **"Pioneering Advances for AI Driverless Cars"** by Dr. Lance Eliot

15. **"Leading Edge Trends for AI Driverless Cars"** by Dr. Lance Eliot

16. **"The Cutting Edge of AI Autonomous Cars"** by Dr. Lance Eliot

17. **"The Next Wave of AI Self-Driving Cars"** by Dr. Lance Eliot

18. **"Revolutionary Innovations of AI Driverless Cars"** by Dr. Lance Eliot

19. **"AI Self-Driving Cars Breakthroughs"** by Dr. Lance Eliot

20. **"Trailblazing Trends for AI Self-Driving Cars"** by Dr. Lance Eliot

All of the above books are available on Amazon and at other major global booksellers.

CHAPTER 1

ELIOT FRAMEWORK FOR AI SELF-DRIVING CARS

CHAPTER 1

ELIOT FRAMEWORK FOR AI SELF-DRIVING CARS

This chapter is a core foundational aspect for understanding AI self-driving cars and I have used this same chapter in several of my other books to introduce the reader to essential elements of this field. Once you've read this chapter, you'll be prepared to read the rest of the material since the foundational essence of the components of autonomous AI driverless self-driving cars will have been established for you.

––––––––––

When I give presentations about self-driving cars and teach classes on the topic, I have found it helpful to provide a framework around which the various key elements of self-driving cars can be understood and organized (see diagram at the end of this chapter). The framework needs to be simple enough to convey the overarching elements, but at the same time not so simple that it belies the true complexity of self-driving cars. As such, I am going to describe the framework here and try to offer in a thousand words (or more!) what the framework diagram itself intends to portray.

The core elements on the diagram are numbered for ease of reference. The numbering does not suggest any kind of prioritization of the elements. Each element is crucial. Each element has a purpose, and otherwise would not be included in the framework. For some self-driving cars, a particular element might be more important or somehow distinguished in comparison to other self-driving cars.

You could even use the framework to rate a particular self-driving car, doing so by gauging how well it performs in each of the elements of the framework. I will describe each of the elements, one at a time. After doing so, I'll discuss aspects that illustrate how the elements interact and perform during the overall effort of a self-driving car.

At the Cybernetic Self-Driving Car Institute, we use the framework to keep track of what we are working on, and how we are developing software that fills in what is needed to achieve Level 5 self-driving cars.

D-01: Sensor Capture

Let's start with the one element that often gets the most attention in the press about self-driving cars, namely, the sensory devices for a self-driving car.

On the framework, the box labeled as D-01 indicates "Sensor Capture" and refers to the processes of the self-driving car that involve collecting data from the myriad of sensors that are used for a self-driving car. The types of devices typically involved are listed, such as the use of mono cameras, stereo cameras, LIDAR devices, radar systems, ultrasonic devices, GPS, IMU, and so on.

These devices are tasked with obtaining data about the status of the self-driving car and the world around it. Some of the devices are continually providing updates, while others of the devices await an indication by the self-driving car that the device is supposed to collect data. The data might be first transformed in some fashion by the device itself, or it might instead be fed directly into the sensor capture as raw data. At that point, it might be up to the sensor capture processes to do transformations on the data. This all varies depending upon the nature of the devices being used and how the devices were designed and developed.

D-02: Sensor Fusion

Imagine that your eyeballs receive visual images, your nose receives odors, your ears receive sounds, and in essence each of your distinct sensory devices is getting some form of input. The input befits the nature of the device. Likewise, for a self-driving car, the cameras provide visual images, the radar returns radar reflections, and so on.

Each device provides the data as befits what the device does.

At some point, using the analogy to humans, you need to merge together what your eyes see, what your nose smells, what your ears hear, and piece it all together into a larger sense of what the world is all about and what is happening around you. Sensor fusion is the action of taking the singular aspects from each of the devices and putting them together into a larger puzzle.

Sensor fusion is a tough task. There are some devices that might not be working at the time of the sensor capture. Or, there might some devices that are unable to report well what they have detected. Again, using a human analogy, suppose you are in a dark room and so your eyes cannot see much. At that point, you might need to rely more so on your ears and what you hear. The same is true for a self-driving car. If the cameras are obscured due to snow and sleet, it might be that the radar can provide a greater indication of what the external conditions consist of.

In the case of a self-driving car, there can be a plethora of such sensory devices. Each is reporting what it can. Each might have its difficulties. Each might have its limitations, such as how far ahead it can detect an object. All of these limitations need to be considered during the sensor fusion task.

D-03: Virtual World Model

For humans, we presumably keep in our minds a model of the world around us when we are driving a car. In your mind, you know that the car is going at say 60 miles per hour and that you are on a freeway. You have a model in your mind that your car is surrounded by other cars, and that there are lanes to the freeway. Your model is not only based on what you can see, hear, etc., but also what you know about the nature of the world. You know that at any moment that car ahead of you can smash on its brakes, or the car behind you can ram into your car, or that the truck in the next lane might swerve into your lane.

The AI of the self-driving car needs to have a virtual world model, which it then keeps updated with whatever it is receiving from the sensor fusion, which received its input from the sensor capture and the sensory devices.

D-04: System Action Plan

By having a virtual world model, the AI of the self-driving car is able to keep track of where the car is and what is happening around the car. In addition, the AI needs to determine what to do next. Should the self-driving car hit its brakes? Should the self-driving car stay in its lane or swerve into the lane to the left? Should the self-driving car accelerate or slow down?

A system action plan needs to be prepared by the AI of the self-driving car. The action plan specifies what actions should be taken. The actions need to pertain to the status of the virtual world model. Plus, the actions need to be realizable.

This realizability means that the AI cannot just assert that the self-driving car should suddenly sprout wings and fly. Instead, the AI must be bound by whatever the self-driving car can actually do, such as coming to a halt in a distance of X feet at a speed of Y miles per hour, rather than perhaps asserting that the self-driving car come to a halt in 0 feet as though it could instantaneously come to a stop while it is in motion.

D-05: Controls Activation

The system action plan is implemented by activating the controls of the car to act according to what the plan stipulates. This might mean that the accelerator control is commanded to increase the speed of the car. Or, the steering control is commanded to turn the steering wheel 30 degrees to the left or right.

One question arises as to whether or not the controls respond as they are commanded to do. In other words, suppose the AI has commanded the accelerator to increase, but for some reason it does not do so. Or, maybe it tries to do so, but the speed of the car does not increase. The controls activation feeds back into the virtual world model, and simultaneously the virtual world model is getting updated from the sensors, the sensor capture, and the sensor fusion. This allows the AI to ascertain what has taken place as a result of the controls being commanded to take some kind of action.

By the way, please keep in mind that though the diagram seems to have a linear progression to it, the reality is that these are all aspects of the self-driving car that are happening in parallel and simultaneously. The sensors are capturing data, meanwhile the sensor fusion is taking place, meanwhile the virtual model is being updated, meanwhile the system action plan is being formulated and reformulated, meanwhile the controls are being activated.

This is the same as a human being that is driving a car. They are eyeballing the road, meanwhile they are fusing in their mind the sights, sounds, etc., meanwhile their mind is updating their model of the world around them, meanwhile they are formulating an action plan of what to do, and meanwhile they are pushing their foot onto the pedals and steering the car. In the normal course of driving a car, you are doing all of these at once. I mention this so that when you look at the diagram, you will think of the boxes as processes that are all happening at the same time, and not as though only one happens and then the next.

They are shown diagrammatically in a simplistic manner to help comprehend what is taking place. You though should also realize that they are working in parallel and simultaneous with each other. This is a tough aspect in that the inter-element communications involve latency and other aspects that must be taken into account. There can be delays in one element updating and then sharing its latest status with other elements.

D-06: Automobile & CAN

Contemporary cars use various automotive electronics and a Controller Area Network (CAN) to serve as the components that underlie the driving aspects of a car. There are Electronic Control Units (ECU's) which control subsystems of the car, such as the engine, the brakes, the doors, the windows, and so on.

The elements D-01, D-02, D-03, D-04, D-05 are layered on top of the D-06, and must be aware of the nature of what the D-06 is able to do and not do.

D-07: In-Car Commands

Humans are going to be occupants in self-driving cars. In a Level 5 self-driving car, there must be some form of communication that takes place between the humans and the self-driving car. For example, I go into a self-driving car and tell it that I want to be driven over to Disneyland, and along the way I want to stop at In-and-Out Burger. The self-driving car now parses what I've said and tries to then establish a means to carry out my wishes.

In-car commands can happen at any time during a driving journey. Though my example was about an in-car command when I first got into my self-driving car, it could be that while the self-driving car is carrying out the journey that I change my mind. Perhaps after getting stuck in traffic, I tell the self-driving car to forget about getting the burgers and just head straight over to the theme park. The self-driving car needs to be alert to in-car commands throughout the journey.

D-08: V2X Communications

We will ultimately have self-driving cars communicating with each other, doing so via V2V (Vehicle-to-Vehicle) communications. We will also have self-driving cars that communicate with the roadways and other aspects of the transportation infrastructure, doing so via V2I (Vehicle-to-Infrastructure).

The variety of ways in which a self-driving car will be communicating with other cars and infrastructure is being called V2X, whereby the letter X means whatever else we identify as something that a car should or would want to communicate with. The V2X communications will be taking place simultaneous with everything else on the diagram, and those other elements will need to incorporate whatever it gleans from those V2X communications.

D-09: Deep Learning

The use of Deep Learning permeates all other aspects of the self-driving car. The AI of the self-driving car will be using deep learning to do a better job at the systems action plan, and at the controls activation, and at the sensor fusion, and so on.

Currently, the use of artificial neural networks is the most prevalent form of deep learning. Based on large swaths of data, the neural networks attempt to "learn" from the data and therefore direct the efforts of the self-driving car accordingly.

D-10: Tactical AI

Tactical AI is the element of dealing with the moment-to-moment driving of the self-driving car. Is the self-driving car staying in its lane of the freeway? Is the car responding appropriately to the controls commands? Are the sensory devices working?

For human drivers, the tactical equivalent can be seen when you watch a novice driver such as a teenager that is first driving. They are focused on the mechanics of the driving task, keeping their eye on the road while also trying to properly control the car.

D-11: Strategic AI

The Strategic AI aspects of a self-driving car are dealing with the larger picture of what the self-driving car is trying to do. If I had asked that the self-driving car take me to Disneyland, there is an overall journey map that needs to be kept and maintained.

There is an interaction between the Strategic AI and the Tactical AI. The Strategic AI is wanting to keep on the mission of the driving, while the Tactical AI is focused on the particulars underway in the driving effort. If the Tactical AI seems to wander away from the overarching mission, the Strategic AI wants to see why and get things back on track. If the Tactical AI realizes that there is something amiss on the self-driving car, it needs to alert the Strategic AI accordingly and have an adjustment to the overarching mission that is underway.

D-12: Self-Aware AI

Very few of the self-driving cars being developed are including a Self-Aware AI element, which we at the Cybernetic Self-Driving Car Institute believe is crucial to Level 5 self-driving cars.

The Self-Aware AI element is intended to watch over itself, in the sense that the AI is making sure that the AI is working as intended. Suppose you had a human driving a car, and they were starting to drive erratically. Hopefully, their own self-awareness would make them realize they themselves are driving poorly, such as perhaps starting to fall asleep after having been driving for hours on end. If you had a passenger in the car, they might be able to alert the driver if the driver is starting to do something amiss. This is exactly what the Self-Aware

AI element tries to do, it becomes the overseer of the AI, and tries to detect when the AI has become faulty or confused, and then find ways to overcome the issue.

D-13: Economic

The economic aspects of a self-driving car are not per se a technology aspect of a self-driving car, but the economics do indeed impact the nature of a self-driving car. For example, the cost of outfitting a self-driving car with every kind of possible sensory device is prohibitive, and so choices need to be made about which devices are used. And, for those sensory devices chosen, whether they would have a full set of features or a more limited set of features.

We are going to have self-driving cars that are at the low-end of a consumer cost point, and others at the high-end of a consumer cost point. You cannot expect that the self-driving car at the low-end is going to be as robust as the one at the high-end. I realize that many of the self-driving car pundits are acting as though all self-driving cars will be the same, but they won't be. Just like anything else, we are going to have self-driving cars that have a range of capabilities. Some will be better than others. Some will be safer than others. This is the way of the real-world, and so we need to be thinking about the economics aspects when considering the nature of self-driving cars.

D-14: Societal

This component encompasses the societal aspects of AI which also impacts the technology of self-driving cars. For example, the famous Trolley Problem involves what choices should a self-driving car make when faced with life-and-death matters. If the self-driving car is about to either hit a child standing in the roadway, or instead ram into a tree at the side of the road and possibly kill the humans in the self-driving car, which choice should be made?

We need to keep in mind the societal aspects will underlie the AI of the self-driving car. Whether we are aware of it explicitly or not, the AI will have embedded into it various societal assumptions.

D-15: Innovation

I included the notion of innovation into the framework because we can anticipate that whatever a self-driving car consists of, it will continue to be innovated over time. The self-driving cars coming out in the next several years will undoubtedly be different and less innovative than the versions that come out in ten years hence, and so on.

Framework Overall

For those of you that want to learn about self-driving cars, you can potentially pick a particular element and become specialized in that aspect. Some engineers are focusing on the sensory devices. Some engineers focus on the controls activation. And so on. There are specialties in each of the elements.

Researchers are likewise specializing in various aspects. For example, there are researchers that are using Deep Learning to see how best it can be used for sensor fusion. There are other researchers that are using Deep Learning to derive good System Action Plans. Some are studying how to develop AI for the Strategic aspects of the driving task, while others are focused on the Tactical aspects.

A well-prepared all-around software developer that is involved in self-driving cars should be familiar with all of the elements, at least to the degree that they know what each element does. This is important since whatever piece of the pie that the software developer works on, they need to be knowledgeable about what the other elements are doing.

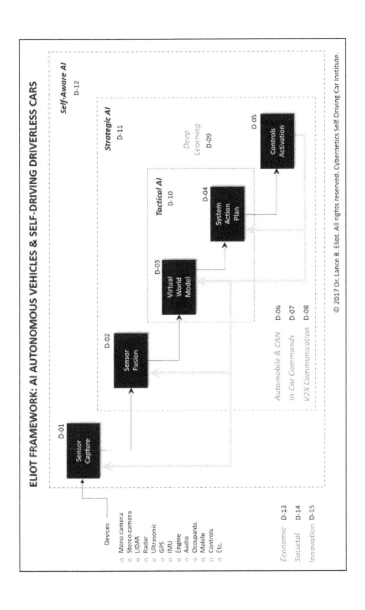

ELIOT FRAMEWORK: AI AUTONOMOUS VEHICLES & SELF-DRIVING DRIVERLESS CARS

CHAPTER 2

STRATEGIC AI METAPHORS AND AI SELF-DRIVING CARS

CHAPTER 2

STRATEGIC AI METAPHORS
AND AI SELF-DRIVING CARS

For leaders overseeing any substantive AI initiative, it is crucial to establish a strategic vision of what you are ultimately trying to achieve. The strategic vision should layout the nature of the AI system that you are embarking upon creating and has to be relatively clear cut so that anyone involved will readily grasp your aims.

If you fail to identify a strategic vision for the AI effort, the odds are that few will comprehend what you are seeking to build and field. Without a collective understanding among your AI developers, you can end up with something that goes astray of your intention. Worse still, if the overall direction and purpose is muddled or not defined at all, you could wind-up with an untoward result, having wasted precious resources and time that otherwise might have led to better success.

A strategic vision for your AI project can consist of a narrative that spells out in some detail the goals and objectives, plus it is handy to have a pictorial representation that can visually depict your wordy description. Though a description and a picture are worthy, you might also find that making use of a metaphor can be a very powerful communicative mechanism too.

Metaphors are used all the time for major initiatives. Sports metaphors are particularly popular. The leader responsible for a major systems effort might cast the effort in say baseball sporting terms. Let's try to hit one over the fence, they might say. We are putting together an AI system that will get us to the world series and beyond, a leader might exclaim. If they are more of a football fan, they might indicate that the project is going to be a big touchdown for the company and advance the field of AI.

You've got to be somewhat careful though when you start invoking metaphors. There is a potential two-way street about a metaphor. The metaphor can support your efforts and be a quick-and-easy means to convey the spirit and excitement involved in the AI initiative. On the other hand, there are doubters and cynics that might try to turnaround the metaphor and use it against the AI project, especially if the AI system is having troubles during the development stage.

I recall one AI project that the leader used a football metaphor and had posters made-up that were placed onto the walls where the AI development team was working. At first, the football aspects were embraced and used by the developers. Some even brought into the office a football helmet and had it marked with the company name and logo. Team spirit, rallies, and the like, all helped to get the effort launched.

Unfortunately, as the project began to hit bottlenecks, and it was starting to look unlikely that they could achieve the AI capabilities envisioned, some said that the AI system had become a Hail Mary kind of effort. A Hail Mary in football is a long-distance forward pass that is usually made in utter desperation. When a football team realizes that they cannot otherwise score in a more reasoned manner, they at times might resort to the high-risk low-odds Hail Mary tactic. In that sense, the AI project had become a Hail Mary, something that few now believed would succeed and at best they might make a frantic last-resort final-ditch scuffle to revive.

In spite of the chances that a metaphor might be turned against an AI effort, it is likely better to have a metaphor than to not have one. If your major AI project does not have an "officially" anointed metaphor that you've carefully chosen, it provides a vacuum into which others might offer a worse-choice metaphor anyway.

One of the most commonly evoked vacuum-filling metaphor's for AI projects is the Frankenstein metaphor. We all already know about Frankenstein, or at least we've all heard of Frankenstein, regardless whether you've read Mary Shelley's book or seen a movie that decently covers her novel. By and large, most people have formed an image that Frankenstein refers to something that has been put together piecemeal, tossing together various parts, and the end-result is usually considered evil or certainly at least ill-advised.

Frankenstein is a rather "sticky" kind of metaphor for especially AI projects, and once your AI effort has been tainted by it, you'll have a relatively hard time removing the stench.

The reason that Frankenstein is so sticky for AI projects is that it seems to fit well if you consider what an AI system is about. Frankenstein was brought to life, and in some respects there is an appealingly apt association with AI systems that are bringing something to life (though, obviously not in the same biological sense as Frankenstein). If people in your firm or even outside of your firm begin to assert that your AI system is some kind of Frankenstein, you are probably headed downhill on it or perhaps are already at the bottom of a hole you'll not dig out of.

The metaphor that you choose has to be readily grasped by those that are going to be guided by it. If you pick something obscure as your metaphor, you'll be spending most of your time just trying to explain what you mean. For example, one AI leader opted to tell his team that they were embarking upon building the Bismarck.

I dare say that most AI developers that are in the Gen Z age bracket are probably either not aware of the Bismarck or at best have the vaguest notion of what it was. During World War II, the German's built a massive battleship, which they named the Bismarck, and it became famous at the time for its power and prestige. Eventually, it got into a tussle with Allie ships that were trying to sink it, and the German commander of the ship opted to scuttle and sink the Bismarck, so it would not get into the hands of the Allies.

The leader of the AI group was from the Baby Boomer era and thus he was more so connected to World War II history via his father that had served during WWII. In the mind of this AI group leader, he thought that everyone knew about the Bismarck. For him, casting the AI system as the Bismarck was handy because it was an AI autonomous vehicle that was going to be used in the water, and using a ship metaphor seemed to be relevant and clever.

When I chatted with members of his AI team, many were in their early 20's and recent college grads, several sheepishly told me that they had to look-up the Bismarck to know what it was. And though they appreciated the idea behind the metaphor, it fell flat from their perspective (it was too outdated of a metaphor, and for which they felt that this outdatedness was going to be inadvertently reflected on the AI system, even though the AI system was modern-day and state-of-the-art).

There was even scuttlebutt behind the AI leader's back that maybe he should have used the Titanic as the metaphor, due to the aspect that they were having massive problems getting the AI system to work. Some were worried that the project was going to fail and "sink" their careers with it. This further illustrates the two-sided coin of using metaphors.

Besides considering whether a chosen metaphor will resonate with your targeted audience, you also need to include the cultural aspects that might come to play too.

There is an effort afoot by a start-up seeking to create a drone-based network in Africa to deliver medical supplies. The use of drones seems particularly applicable as they might be a low-cost and largely effective means to reach remote areas of Africa. In hopes of overcoming qualms that the public might have about a vast set of drones flying back-and-forth across the continent over their heads, which might have a military related connotation as something troublesome, the start-up refers to the drone network as flying donkeys, a metaphor they conjured up.

The intent of the flying donkeys metaphor is that you are supposed to right away envision that a donkey is something good and therefore the drone network gets that goodly glow. We all readily know that donkeys are used to carry loads of goods and often do so for long distances, tirelessly and faithfully doing so. Unless you've been kicked by a donkey, you probably have a positive image of donkeys.

By saying that the donkeys are flying, you capture the essence of the drones that are going to be flying, and you also generate a catchy imaginary. The founder believes this metaphor is apt and appeals to his target audience.

I'd like to leave that matter there, but I suppose I should also mention that some that are disbelievers and doubt that the drone network will ever get going, they say the day they will have a fully functioning flying donkey network is the same day that there will be flying pigs (which, if you don't know, flying pigs is an expression usually meaning that something will never happen). This once again shows the two-sided potential advantage and also disadvantage of using a metaphor for your project.

What does this have to do with AI self-driving cars?

At the Cybernetic AI Self-Driving Car Institute, we are developing AI software for self-driving cars. There are some auto makers and tech firms that are using metaphors to help internally or at times externally convey the nature of their AI self-driving car initiatives.

Perhaps the most frequently used metaphor is the Knight Rider KITT, which I'll explain what that is and offer both the positive and negative aspects of using this particular metaphor.

I'd like to first clarify and introduce the notion that there are varying levels of AI self-driving cars. The topmost level is considered Level 5. A Level 5 self-driving car is one that is being driven by the AI and there is no human driver involved. For the design of Level 5 self-driving cars, the auto makers are even removing the gas pedal, brake pedal, and steering wheel, since those are contraptions used by human drivers. The Level 5 self-driving car is not being driven by a human and nor is there an expectation that a human driver will be present in the self-driving car. It's all on the shoulders of the AI to drive the car.

For self-driving cars less than a Level 5, there must be a human driver present in the car. The human driver is currently considered the responsible party for the acts of the car. The AI and the human driver are co-sharing the driving task. In spite of this co-sharing, the human is supposed to remain fully immersed into the driving task and be ready at all times to perform the driving task. I've repeatedly warned about the dangers of this co-sharing arrangement and predicted it will produce many untoward results.

Let's focus herein on the true Level 5 self-driving car. Much of the comments apply to the less than Level 5 self-driving cars too, but the fully autonomous AI self-driving car will receive the most attention in this discussion.

Here's the usual steps involved in the AI driving task:

- Sensor data collection and interpretation

- Sensor fusion

- Virtual world model updating

- AI action planning

- Car controls command issuance

Another key aspect of AI self-driving cars is that they will be driving on our roadways in the midst of human driven cars too. There are some pundits of AI self-driving cars that continually refer to a utopian world in which there are only AI self-driving cars on the public roads. Currently there are about 250+ million conventional cars in the United States alone, and those cars are not going to magically disappear or become true Level 5 AI self-driving cars overnight.

Indeed, the use of human driven cars will last for many years, likely many decades, and the advent of AI self-driving cars will occur while there are still human driven cars on the roads. This is a crucial point since this means that the AI of self-driving cars needs to be able to contend with not just other AI self-driving cars, but also contend with human driven cars. It is easy to envision a simplistic and rather unrealistic world in which all AI self-driving cars are politely interacting with each other and being civil about roadway interactions. That's not what is going to be happening for the foreseeable future. AI self-driving cars and human driven cars will need to be able to cope with each other.

Returning to the topic of metaphors used for AI self-driving cars by some auto makers and tech firms, the most prevalent one seems to be undertaken by making reference to the Knight Rider KITT.

Knight Rider is the name of a TV series and an entertainment franchise that first launched in the early 1980s. The original TV series ran from 1982 to 1986. There was a later resurgence of interest including a series of movies made and released, video games, and as a gradually emerging pop culture icon the TV series was rebooted several times during the 1990s and the 2000's.

The fictional plot of the Knight Rider series is that a man named Michael Knight makes use of a "partner" in his efforts to fight crime, of which the partner is his car. The car is imbued with AI and is made by the fictional Knight Industries company. The model number of the AI-based car is the model 2000, and thus the clever name of the car is the Knight Industries Two Thousand or "KITT" for short. Later on, there was a newer model, the Three Thousand, but this conveniently also can be called KITT too.

I would guess that anyone that is really enamored of the Knight Rider KITT is familiar with the 1982 Pontiac Firebird that was used in the original TV series. A wide variety of other cars were used in subsequent stages of the TV and film adaptations. I admit that when I see a picture of a Pontiac Firebird or a restored one, I instantly think of KITT. Hope this doesn't seemingly date me.

One question that comes up about using the Knight Rider KITT as a metaphor for building today's AI self-driving cars involves whether your AI developers are familiar with KITT. On the one hand, it is somewhat outdated since it got started in the early 1980s. On the other hand, the numerous reboots and avenues through which KITT is deployed such as video games, keeps it somewhat contemporary or at least increases awareness more so than if it had existed only in the original TV series and had not gotten reinvigorated over and over.

It's also interesting that though some people know what you mean when you say "Knight Rider," of which they associate the car to that phrasing, if you also say to them "KITT" it is less likely they seem to know what KITT means. They might have heard of "KITT" and thought it meant "Kit" as in a kit that turns a car into an AI-based car. Rarer is the person that knows the letters of K.I.T.T. are an acronym and nor what the acronym consists.

Nevertheless, it doesn't matter much whether someone knows what KITT means and nor whether they "Knight Rider" phrase is not the name of the car per se. All that really matters is that they know that either Knight Rider or KITT refers to an AI-based car. That's sufficient.

As a crime fighter, Michael Knight drives around in KITT and interacts with the car as though it is a human being. KITT is supposedly making use of a cybernetic processor and the system was transplanted from a mainframe AI-computer that was being used by the United States government. Michael Knight is the heroic everyday human crime fighter (no super powers), and he is aided by his trusty horse, well, actually, trusty car, and the AI of the car is able to help him reason about the crime fighting and capture the criminals they are seeking.

Put yourself back into the 1980s era and the description of KITT makes a lot of sense for that time period. During the 1980's, it was commonplace to refer to AI systems as being cybernetic. Also, we mainly had large mainframe computers and the advent of PC's was just in its infancy (the IBM PC launched in 1981, the Apple Mac in 1984). The fiction writers that composed the Knight Rider series were using the terminology of the time period in coming up with the KITT backstory.

One nifty aspect of using the Knight Rider KITT metaphor is that the plotline involved good guys and fighting crime. In that sense, the imagery of KITT the car is a quite positive one. It was trying to be a do gooder. It worked well with humans, at least ones on the right side of the law. It was loyal to its human "master" which was Michael Knight. These are all facets of the AI-based car that make it palatable for use as a metaphor today.

Suppose that KITT was evil and wantonly killed people. Suppose that KITT was wanting to takeover humanity. Suppose that KITT disobeyed its human master and was AI uncontrolled. All of those aspects would reflect on what we envision when you invoke the Knight Rider KITT metaphor. Instead, it is a squeaky clean metaphor and one that involves heroics. Score one for the use of the KITT metaphor.

You might try to use some other famous "talking cars" for your metaphor, but the pickings are rather slim. There is the "My Mother the Car" TV series that ran in the 1960s. That's ancient times today, and thus it is relatively buried now in history. Plus, the car was a decrepit 1928 Porter touring car. I don't think any modern auto maker or tech firm wants that imagery.

You could try invoking Herbie, the AI-based VW Beetle that starred in the Disney 1968 motion picture "The Love Bug." Herbie has had a rather lengthy life span as a franchise, mainly in films and at the Disney parks. It was cute. It was cuddly. You could try to use it as a metaphor for today's AI-based cars, which might be handy to suggest that AI-based cars are friendly and lovable. Again, doubtful any auto maker or tech firm would want that image per se for their AI self-driving car.

Generally, the sleek and cool aspects of the Knight Rider KITT provide a top choice for serving as a metaphor for today's AI self-driving car makers and what they are trying to achieve. It is a tad outdated but not much, it invokes a heroic image, and the AI was "manageable" and not out of control.

Let's consider further the AI aspects of KITT.

Using the fictional Knight 2000 microprocessor, the fictional car had a fictional Voice Synthesizer and a Etymotic Equalizer (audio input) to interact with humans. You might famously recall that this consisted of either a flashing red square inside the car or a three section vertical bats that flashed when the car was speaking. This visual device was used to get those of us watching the show to realize that the car was speaking. If the flashing light trickery had not been used, it might have been less believable that the car was speaking. You'd be looking around for where is that voice coming from.

For the emerging AI self-driving cars, there's no question that voice interaction is going to be crucial. Human occupants that are passengers in a true Level 5 self-driving car will interact verbally with the AI system. This includes not just commands of where they want to go, but actually much more complex interactions. The AI will need to be savvy enough to interact about desired aspects of how the human wants the car to drive, where it is driving too, and other aspects. In that sense, KITT hit the mark.

The use of the flashing lights to represent when KITT was talking is something that will arise for AI self-driving cars too. Humans are used to speaking to other humans by facing the human and seeing their lips and mouth move. Even when we drive-up to a fast food drive-thru, we look for the speaker and assume that's where we need to speak back. Designers of AI self-driving cars can either just let human occupants look around confusedly for where to speak to, or put some kind of "obvious" audio input device in say the dashboard. I realize that the inside of an AI self-driving car will likely be lined with several audio input devices and so the humans don't have to speak in a specific direction per se, but to make things clearer for humans it might make sense to provide a focal point for when they try to talk to the AI.

KITT had a wide variety of sensory devices to figure out the driving scene and how to navigate along streets and highways. For Level 5 self-driving cars, we're currently using a wide variety of sensory devices, including cameras, radar, ultra-sonic, LIDAR, sonar, and so on.

It is handy that KITT likewise uses sensory devices, since if it just magically knew about its surroundings this would undermine to some extent the fit of the metaphor to AI self-driving cars.

KITT though went a bit further with the sensory devices than we are today. It used X-rays and other somewhat exotic sensory devices.

One such "exotic" sensory device that I've been advocating and exploring is the use of an olfactory sensor for detecting odors. Coincidentally KITT had one.

There is a compelling use case for having an olfactory sensory device in an AI self-driving car. I know that some might think it questionable or fluff, and it is considered an edge or corner case at best right now by most auto makers and tech firms. I claim and have made the case that this will be something of value and a future differentiator for those auto makers or tech firms that opt to include it in their AI self-driving car offerings.

KITT also had a money dispenser so that Michael Knight could get cash when he needed it. ATM's in the early 1980s were still somewhat of a novelty and thus the idea of the KITT having its own internal ATM for Michael Knight was clever and handy. For Level 5 self-driving cars, I've predicted that they will be using blockchain for cryptocurrency use, allowing the human passengers to carry on electronic or digital cash transactions. No need to have a cash dispensing ATM inside a Level 5 AI self-driving car.

One area that the metaphor to KITT perhaps is not quite fully applicable involves the crime fighting capabilities of the car.

KITT had a special armored plating that protected it from bullets and explosions. Though this might the case for Level 5 self-driving cars far off in the future, or maybe for militarized versions of self-driving cars in the nearer term, I don't think we'll be seeing auto makers outfitting everyday AI self-driving cars with the molecular bonded shell (or similar) that KITT used.

Here's some additional aspects that I doubt we'll see in everyday AI self-driving cars that KITT had for crime fighting purposes:

- Could create a smoke screen and lay down slick oil to dissuade cars chasing it (I've seen conventional cars today that do this simply because they are leaking oil!)

- Had a flame thrower (I realize that Elon Musk really likes flame throwers, but I doubt we'll see them in Tesla's any time soon)

- Tear gas launcher

- Lasers to burn through steel plates and walls

- Bomb sniffer

- Seat ejection system (like James Bond had!)

- Other

Some of those crime fighting items are perhaps humorous to note but do keep in mind that if you invoke the Knight Rider KITT as a metaphor, there are some people that might wonder whether or not you are intending to include those kinds of defensive and offensive weapons.

As mentioned earlier, it could make sense to include such capabilities on perhaps military self-driving vehicles or perhaps police self-driving cars. Thus, it is not beyond the realm of "reasonableness" for some to wonder whether your use of the metaphor extends to those aspects too. You probably would want to make sure to clarify when you invoke the Knight Rider KITT metaphor whether you are also encompassing these auxiliary crime fighting kinds of features.

KITT had a Telephone Comlink that allowed the car and Michael Knight to talk with other people on the phone. Of course, we nowadays have cell phones and in the 1980s it was a rather unusual aspect to have a phone capability of any kind available in your car. The Telephone Comlink in that era seemed quite extraordinary and futuristic. How time flies!

For true Level 5 self-driving cars, they will likely be outfitted with various electronic communications and networking capabilities. There will be OTA, Over-The-Air, capabilities for the AI to communicate with the cloud of the auto maker or tech firm. This will allow for the pushing of collected sensory data up to the cloud, along with the auto maker being able to push down into the AI the latest system updates and patches for it. There will also be V2V (vehicle-to-vehicle) electronic communications and V2I (vehicle-to-infrastructure) electronic communications.

The part of the KITT car that drove the car was called the Alpha Circuit. This is kind of interesting because Tesla calls their AI-component the AutoPilot. Most of the auto makers and tech firms are giving specific names to the AI-based element of their self-driving cars. As an aside, I've often indicated in my other articles and my speeches that the industry needs to be mindful and cautious of the names they give to their AI-based component.

I say this because, in short, the name of the AI-based component is another example of a two-sided coin. Coming up with a catchy name for the AI is useful and can be a boon to marketing of an AI self-driving car. On the other hand, it can boomerang in that if the name perhaps implies a greater AI capability than truly exists, there might be backlash against the name. In the case of Tesla, I've mentioned that the use of "AutoPilot" has already spurred some lawsuits as to the implications of the naming for consumers that bought the Tesla cars outfitted with the feature.

KITT came with a turbo booster.

Michael Knight could ramp-up the speed to a top of around 200" miles per hour (including going forward and for going backwards). Do not be expecting the everyday AI self-driving car to go that fast, at least not for the foreseeable future.

I have though predicted that we'll be seeing AI self-driving cars that go at high-speeds on purposely wide-open highways as a potential alternative to building expensive high-speed rails to transport people.

There were several driving modes of KITT.

In one mode, Normal Cruise, the human driver, Michael Knight, was driving the car. Meanwhile, KITT was watching the driving and could take over the driving task as needed. In another mode, Auto Cruise, KITT was a like a true Level 5 self-driving car that could autonomously drive the car and not need any human driving input or assistance.

There was also a Pursuit mode, used for crime fighting purposes. I know that this mode seems like the antithesis of what most AI developers are thinking about when it comes to AI self-driving cars. In the view of these AI developers, they imagine a Utopian world in which there will no longer be any kind of high-speed pursuits. I've debunked this notion. There will be circumstances where a "pursuit" mode makes sense and would be an aspect desired and needed by even law-abiding AI self-driving cars.

There are other various capabilities of KITT and in the later years of the series the features seemed to get rather extravagant. The writers of the series likely were under pressure to come up with new gimmicks and keep things fresh.

On a related matter for true Level 5 AI self-driving cars, at first they will have a core set of capabilities and we'll likely all be pleased and excited to have those core features. Once the general public gets comfortable using an AI self-driving car, I'm sure that there will be a features-war by the auto makers and tech firms to try and differentiate one self-driving car model from another.

In that sense, some of the more "extravagant" items of KITT might actually be later designed, built and added to future models of true Level 5 AI self-driving cars. I'm not referring to the laser beams that destroy things (let's hope we don't all end-up with such a feature), but more so the olfactory sensors, the medical status scanners that KITT had, and so on.

Conclusion

Using a metaphor to label an AI systems project can be quite powerful as a means to establish the strategic vision for what you are aiming to achieve. Make sure you pick a relevant metaphor. Try to avoid picking one that is hard for people to comprehend or that is outdated or otherwise seemingly lacks stickiness and relevance. Be on the watch for efforts to distort or twist the metaphor, which, if that happens, it could also be a warning sign that your AI project is drifting into a potential abyss and you ought to be cognizant of that slippage.

For AI self-driving cars, the use of the Knight Rider KITT metaphor is handy and offers some significant advantages. The Knight Rider car enjoys a rather positive impression already, and this can carry over into your AI self-driving car effort. Make sure to clarify what aspects are relevant and which are not, otherwise you might end-up with a passenger car that can launch missiles and ram through walls.

Admittedly, since my daily commute on the freeway in Los Angeles takes about 1 to 2 hours due to snarled traffic, I'd welcome having those missile launchers and ramming features on my AI self-driving car. But, only on mine, and not on anyone else's. That's personalization of AI self-driving cars.

CHAPTER 3
EMERGENCY-ONLY AI
AND
AI SELF-DRIVING CARS

CHAPTER 3

EMERGENCY-ONLY AI
AND
AI SELF-DRIVING CARS

I had just fallen asleep in my hotel room when the fire alarm rang out. It was a few minutes past 2 a.m. and the hotel was relatively full and mainly had been quiet at this hour as most of the hotel guests had earlier retired for the evening. The sharp twang of the fire alarm pierced throughout the hallways and walls of the hotel. I could hear the sounds of people moving around in their hotel rooms as they quickly got up to see what was going on.

Just last month I had been staying in a different hotel in a different city and the fire alarm had gone off, but it turned out to be a false alarm. The hotel was a new one that had only been open a few weeks and apparently they were still trying to iron out the bugs of the hotel systems. Somehow, the fire alarm system had gone off, right around midnight, and after a few minutes the hotel staff told everyone not to worry since it was a false alarm.

Of course, some more discerning hotel guests remained worried since they didn't necessarily believe the staff that the fire alarm was a false one. Maybe the staff was wrong, and if so, the consequences could be deadly. Ultimately, there was no apparent sign of a fire, no smoke, no flames, and gradually even the most skeptical of guests went back to sleep.

I could not believe that I was once again hearing a fire alarm. In my many years of staying at hotels while traveling for work and sometimes (rarely) for vacations, I had only experienced a few occasions of a fire alarm ringing out. Now, I had two in a short span of time. The earlier one had been a dud, a false alarm. I figured that perhaps this most recent fire alarm was also a false alarm. But, should I base this assumption on the mere fact that I had a few weeks earlier experienced a false alarm? The logic was not especially iron tight since these were two completely different hotels and had nothing particularly in common, other than that I had stayed at both of them.

The good thing about my recent experience of a false alarm was that it had remained me of the precautions you should undertake when staying at a hotel. As such, I had made sure that my normal routine while staying at hotels incorporated the appropriate fire-related safeguards. One is to have your shoes close to where you can find them when you awakened at night by a fire or a fire alarm, allowing you to quickly put on the shoes for escaping from the room. Without shoes on, you might try to escape the room or run down the hallway and there could be broken items like glass or other shards that would inhibit your escape or harm you as you tried to get out.

I also kept my key personal items such as my wallet and smartphone nearby the bed and had my pants and jacket also ready in case needed. I knew too the path to the doorway of my hotel room and kept it clear of obstructions, doing so before I went to sleep for the night. I had made sure to scrutinize the hallway and knew the nearest exits and where the stairs were. Some people also prefer to stay in the lower floors of a hotel, doing so in case the firefighters are trying to get you out, which they can then more readily reach either by foot or via a firetruck ladder.

I don't want you to think I was obsessed with being ready for an emergency. The precautions I've just mentioned are all easily done without any real extra or extraordinary effort involved. When I first check into my hotel room, I glance around the hallway as I am walking to the room, spotting where the exits and the stairs are. When I go to sleep at night, I make sure the hotel room door is locked and then as I walk back to the bed I then also make sure the path is unobstructed. These are facets that can be done by habit and seamlessly fit in with the effort involved in staying at a hotel.

So, what did I do about the blaring fire alarm on this most recent hotel stay? I decided that it was worthwhile to assume it was a real fire and not a false alarm, putting my safety at the higher bet than the slovenly assumption that I could remain laying in bed and wait to find out if the alarm was true or false. I rapidly got into my pants and jacket, put on my shoes, grabbed my wallet and smartphone from the bed stand, and went straight to the door that led into the hallway. I touched the door to see if it was hot, another kind of precaution in case the fire is right on the other side of the door (you don't want to open a door leading into a fire, of which the air of your room will simply help ignite further and you'll be charred to a crisp).

Feeling no heat on the door, I slowly opened it to peek into the hallway. Believe it or not, there was smoke in the hallway. Thank goodness that I had opted to believe the fire alarm. I stepped into the hallway cautiously. The smoke appeared to be coming from the west end and not from the east end. I figured this implied that wherever the fire was, it might be more so on the west side rather than the east side of the hotel. I began to walk in the easterly direction.

What seemed peculiar was that there was no one else also making their way through the hallway. I was pretty sure that there were people in the other rooms as I had heard them coming to their rooms earlier that evening (often making a bit of noise after likely visiting the hotel bar and having a few drinks there). Were these other people still asleep? How could they not hear the incessant clanging of the fire alarm? The sound was blaring and loud enough to wake the dead.

I decided to bang on the doors of the rooms that I was walking past. I would rap a door with my fist and then yell out "Fire!" to let them know that there was indeed something really happening. My guess was that others had heard the fire alarm but chosen to wait and see what might happen. With the hallway starting to fill with smoke, this seemed sufficient proof to me that a fire was somewhere. The smoke would eventually seep into the rooms. For now, the smoke was mainly floating near the ceiling of the hallway. It wasn't thick enough yet to have filled down to the floor and try to permeate into the rooms at the door seams.

The good news of the situation turned out that no one ended-up getting hurt and the fire was confined to the laundry room of the hotel. The fire department showed-up and put out the flames. They brought in large fans too to help clear out the smoke from the hotel. The staff did an adequate job of helping the hotel guests and moved many of them to another wing of the hotel to get away from the residual smoky smell. It was one of the few times that I'd ever been in a hotel that had a fire and for which I was directly impacted by the fire.

The hotel had smoke alarms in each of the hotel rooms, along with smoke alarms in other areas of the hotel. This is nowadays standard fare for most hotels and also personal residences that you are supposed to have fire alarm devices setup in appropriate areas. These silent guardians are there to be your watchdog. When smoke begins to fill the air, the fire alarm detects the smoke and then starts to beep or clang to alert you.

Some of today's fire alarms speak at you. Rather than simply making a beep sound, these newer fire alarms emit the words "Fire!" or "Get out!" or other kinds of sayings. It is thought that people might be more responsive to hearing what sounds like a human voice telling them what to do. Hearing a beeping sound might not create as strong a response.

You've likely at times wrestled with the fire alarm in your home. Perhaps the fire alarm battery became low and the fire alarm started a low beeping sound to let you know. This often happens on a timed basis wherein the beep sound for the low-battery is at first every say five minutes. If you don't change the battery, the beeping time interval gets reduced. The low-battery beep might then happen every minute, and then every 30 seconds, and so on.

In the hotels that I stay at, they usually also have a fire alarm pull. These are devices typically mounted in the hallways that allow you to grab and pull to alert that a fire is taking place. I'd bet that perhaps when you were in school, someone one time pulled the fire alarm to avoid taking a test. The prankster that pulled the fire alarm is putting everyone at risk, since people can get injured when trying to rush out as a result of hearing a fire alarm, plus it might dull their reaction times the next time there is an actual true fire alarm alert.

Some hotels have a sprinkler system that will spray water to douse a fire. The sprinkler activation might be tied into the fire alarms so that the moment a fire alarm goes off the sprinklers are then activated. This is not usually so closely linked though because of the chances that a false fire alarm might activate the sprinklers. Once those sprinklers start going, it's going to be quite more damaging to the hotel property and you'd obviously want the sprinklers to only go when you are pretty certain that a fire is really occurring. As such, there is often a separate mechanism that has to be operated to get the fire sprinklers to engage.

This discussion about fire alarms and fire protection illuminates some important elements about systems that are designed to help save human lives.

In particular:

- A passive system like the fire alarm pull won't automatically go off and instead the human needs to overtly activate it

- For a passive system, the human needs to be aware of where and how to activate it, else the passive system otherwise does little good to help save the human

- An active system like the smoke alarm is constantly detecting the environment and ready to go off as soon as the conditions occur that will activate the alarm

- Some system elements are intended to simply alert the human and it is then up to the human to take some form of action

- Some system elements such as a fire sprinkler are intended to automatically engage to save human lives and the humans being saved do not need to directly activate the life-saving effort

- These emergency-only systems are intended to be used only when absolutely necessary and otherwise are silent, being somewhat out-of-sight and out-of-mind of most humans

- Such systems are not error-free in that they can at times falsely activate even when there isn't any pending emergency involved

- Humans can undermine these emergency-only systems by not abiding by them or taking other actions that reduce the effectiveness of the system

- Humans will at times distrust an emergency-only system and believe that the system is falsely reporting an emergency and therefore not take prescribed action

I'm invoking the use case of fire alarms as a means to convey the nature of emergency-only systems. There are lots of emergency-only related systems that we might come in contact with in all walks of life. The fire alarm is perhaps the easiest to describe and use as an illustrative aspect to derive the underpinnings of what they do and how humans act and react to them.

What does this have to do with AI self-driving cars?

At the Cybernetic AI Self-Driving Car Institute, we are developing AI software for self-driving cars. One approach that some auto makers and tech firms are taking toward the AI systems for self-driving cars involves designing and implementing those AI systems for emergency-only purposes.

Allow me to elaborate.

I'd like to first clarify and introduce the notion that there are varying levels of AI self-driving cars. The topmost level is considered Level 5. A Level 5 self-driving car is one that is being driven by the AI and there is no human driver involved. For the design of Level 5 self-driving cars, the auto makers are even removing the gas pedal, brake pedal, and steering wheel, since those are contraptions used by human drivers. The Level 5 self-driving car is not being driven by a human and nor is there an expectation that a human driver will be present in the self-driving car. It's all on the shoulders of the AI to drive the car.

For self-driving cars less than a Level 5, there must be a human driver present in the car. The human driver is currently considered the responsible party for the acts of the car. The AI and the human driver are co-sharing the driving task. In spite of this co-sharing, the human is supposed to remain fully immersed into the driving task and be ready at all times to perform the driving task. I've repeatedly warned about the dangers of this co-sharing arrangement and predicted it will produce many untoward results.

Let's focus herein on the true Level 5 self-driving car. Much of the comments apply to the less than Level 5 self-driving cars too, but the fully autonomous AI self-driving car will receive the most attention in this discussion.

Here's the usual steps involved in the AI driving task:
- Sensor data collection and interpretation
- Sensor fusion
- Virtual world model updating
- AI action planning
- Car controls command issuance

Another key aspect of AI self-driving cars is that they will be driving on our roadways in the midst of human driven cars too. There are some pundits of AI self-driving cars that continually refer to a utopian world in which there are only AI self-driving cars on the public roads. Currently there are about 250+ million conventional cars in the United States alone, and those cars are not going to magically disappear or become true Level 5 AI self-driving cars overnight.

Indeed, the use of human driven cars will last for many years, likely many decades, and the advent of AI self-driving cars will occur while there are still human driven cars on the roads. This is a crucial point since this means that the AI of self-driving cars needs to be able to contend with not just other AI self-driving cars, but also contend with human driven cars. It is easy to envision a simplistic and rather unrealistic world in which all AI self-driving cars are politely interacting with each other and being civil about roadway interactions. That's not what is going to be happening for the foreseeable future. AI self-driving cars and human driven cars will need to be able to cope with each other.

Returning to the topic of emergency-only systems, there are various approaches that auto makers and tech firms are taking toward the design and development of AI for self-driving cars and one such approach involves an emergency-only AI paradigm.

As already mentioned, currently the most vaunted and desired approach consists of having the AI always be driving the car and there is no human driving involved at all, which is the intent of a true Level 5 self-driving car. This is much harder to pull off than it might seem. I've variously described this true Level 5 as a kind of moonshot. It's going to take a lot longer to get there than most people seem to think it will.

At the less than Level 5, there is a co-sharing of the driving task. We can step back for a moment and ask an intriguing question about the co-sharing of the driving task, namely, what should the split be between when the AI does the driving and when the human does the driving?

The Level 2 split of human versus AI driving is that the human tends to do the bulk of the driving and the AI tends to do relatively little of the driving task. For the Level 3, the split tends toward having the AI do more so of the driving and the human do less of it. For the Level 4, the amount of driving for the human is further lessened.

Suppose we somewhat turned this split on its head, so to speak. We might design the AI to be an emergency-only kind of mechanism. Rather than the AI driving the self-driving car to varying increasing progressive degrees at the Level 2, Level 3, and Level 4, we might instead opt to have the human be the mainstay driver. The AI would be used for emergency-only purposes.

Let's say I am driving in a Level 3 self-driving car. I would normally be expecting the AI to be the primary driver and I am there in case the AI needs me to take over. I've written and spoken many times about the dangers of this co-sharing arrangement. As a human, I might become complacent and not be ready to take over the driving task when the moment arises for me to do so. Maybe I was playing a video game on my smartphone, maybe I was reading a book that's in my lap, and other kinds of distractions might occur.

Instead of having the AI do most of the driving while in a Level 3, suppose we instead said that the human is the primary driver. The AI is relegated to being an emergency-only driver.

Here's how that might work.

I'm driving my Level 3 car and the AI is quietly observing what is going on. The AI is using all of its sensors to continuously detect and interpret the roadway situation. The sensor fusion is occurring. The virtual world model is being updated. The AI action planning is taking place. The only thing not happening is the issuance of the car controls commands.

In a sense, the AI is for all practical purposes "driving" the car without actually taking over the driving controls. This might be likened to when I was teaching my children how to drive a car. They would sit in the driver's seat. I had no ready means to access the driver controls. Nonetheless, in my head, I was acting as though I was driving the car. I did this to be able to comprehend what my teenage novice driver children were doing and so that I could also come to their aid when needed.

Okay, so the Level 3 car is being driven by the human and all of a sudden another car veers into the lane and threatens to crash into the Level 3 car. We now have a circumstance wherein the human driver of the Level 3 car should presumably take evasive action. Does the human notice that the other car is veering dangerously? Will the human take quick enough action to avoid the crash?

Suppose that the AI was able to ascertain that the veering car is going to crash with the Level 3 car.

Similar to a fire protection system such as at the hotels, the AI can potentially alert the human driver to take action (akin to a fire alarm that belts out an alarm bell).

Or, the AI might take more overt action and momentarily take over the driving controls to maneuver the car away from the danger (this would be somewhat equivalent to the fire sprinklers getting invoked in a hotel).

If the AI was devised to work in an emergency-only mode, some would assert that it relieves the pressure for now on the AI developers to try and devise an all-encompassing AI system that can handle any and all kinds of driving situations. Instead, the AI developers could focus on the emergency-only kinds of situations.

This also would presumably shift attention toward the AI being a kind of hero, stepping into the driving when things are dire and saving the day. Hey, someone might say, the other day the AI of my self-driving car kept me from hitting a dog that ran unexpectedly into the street. Another person might say that the AI saved them from ramming into a car that had come to a sudden halt on the freeway just ahead of their car (and they sheepishly admit they had turned to look at a roadside billboard and by the time they turned their head back the halted car ahead was a surprise).

We are all already somewhat familiar with automated driving assistance systems that can do something similar.

Many cars today have a simplistic detection device that if your car is going to hit something ahead of it, the brakes are automatically applied. These tend to be extremely simplistic in how they work. It is almost a knee-jerk reaction kind of system. There're not much "smarts" involved. You might liken these low-level automated systems as similar to the autonomic nervous system of a human, it reacts instinctively and without much direct thinking involved (when my hand is near a hot stove, presumably my instincts kick-in and I withdraw my hand, doing so without a lot of contemplative effort involved).

These behind-the-scenes automated driving assistance systems would be quietly replaced with a more sophisticated AI-based system that is more robust and paying attention to the overall driving task. The paradigm is that the emergency-only AI is likened to having a second human driver in the car and the secondary driver is there only for emergency driving purposes. The rest of the time, the primary driver is the human that is driving the car.

As mentioned, this might suggest that the AI then does not need to be full-bodied and does not need to be able to drive the car all of the time, and instead be focused on just being able to drive when emergency situations arise. Some would assert though that this is a bit of a paradox. If the AI is not versed enough to be able to drive at any time, how will it be able to discern when an emergency is arising that requires the AI to step into the driving task?

In other words, some would say that only until you have a fully capable driving AI that you would be risking things unduly to have the AI only be used in emergencies. Unless you opted to say that the AI is exclusively used solely in emergencies, you are otherwise suggesting that the AI is able to monitor the driving task throughout and is ready to at any moment do the driving, but if that's the case, why not then let the AI do the driving as the primary driver anyway.

This also brings up the notion of defining the nature of an emergency driving situation. The obvious example of an emergency would be the case of a dog that has darted into the street directly in front of the car and the speed, direction, and timing of the car is such that it will mathematically intersect with the dog if some kind of driving action is not taken to immediately attempt to avoid striking the animal. But this takes us back to the kind of simpleton automated driving assistance systems that are not especially imbued with AI anyway.

If we're going to consider using AI for emergency-only situations, presumably the kinds of emergency situations will range from rather obvious ones that a knee-jerk reactive driving system could handle and all the way up to much more subtle and harder to predict emergencies. If the AI is going to be continuously monitoring the driving situation, we'd want it to be acting like a true secondary driver and be able to do more sophisticated kind of emergency situation detections.

You are on a mountain road that curves back-and-forth. The slow lane has large rambling trucks in it. Your car is in the fast lane that is adjacent to the slow lane. The AI has been observing the slow lane and detected a truck up ahead that periodically has swerved into the fast lane when on a curve. The path of the car is such that in about 10 seconds the car will be passing the truck while on a curve. At this moment there is no apparent danger. But, it can be predicted with sufficient probability that in 10 seconds the likelihood is that the truck will swerve into the lane of the car as it tries to pass the truck on the curve.

Notice that in this example there is not a simple act-react cycle involved. Most of the automated driving assist systems would only react once the car is actually passing the truck and if perchance as the passing action occurred that the truck then veered into the path of the car. Instead, in my example, the AI has anticipated a potential future emergency and will opt to take action beforehand to either prevent the danger or at least be better prepared to cope with it when (if) it occurs.

The emergency-only AI would be presumably boosted beyond the nature of a traditional automated driving assist system, and likely be harkened by the use of Machine Learning (ML). How did the AI even realize that observing the trucks in the slow lane was worthwhile to do? An AI driving system that has learned over time would have the "realization" that trucks often tend to swerve out of their lanes while on curving roads. This then becomes part-and-parcel of the "awareness" that the AI will have when looking for potential emergency driving situations.

Let's now revisit my earlier comments about the nature of emergency-only systems and my illustrative examples of the fire alarm and fire protection systems. I present to you those earlier points and then recast them into the context of AI self-driving cars:

- *A passive system like the fire alarm pull won't automatically go off and instead the human needs to overtly activate it*

Would a driving emergency-only AI system be setup for only a passive mode, meaning that the human driver would need to invoke the AI system? We might have a button that the human could press that invokes the AI emergency capability, or the human might have a "safe word" that they utter to ask the AI to step into the picture.

Downsides with this include that the human might not realize they need or even could use the AI emergency option. Or, the human might realize it but enact the AI emergency mode once it is too late to do anything to avert the incident by the AI.

We would also need to have a means of letting the human know that the AI has "accepted" the inception of going into the AI emergency option mode, otherwise the human might be unsure as to whether or not the AI got the signal and whether the AI is actually stepping into the driving.

There is also the matter of returning the driving back to the human once the emergency action by the AI has been undertaken. How would the AI be able to "know" that the human is prepared to resume driving the car? Would it ask the human driver or just assume that if the human is still at the driver controls that it is Okay to disengage by the AI?

- *For a passive system, the human needs to be aware of where and how to activate it, else the passive system otherwise does little good to help save the human*

As mentioned, a human driver might forget that the AI is standing ready to take over. Plus, when an emergency arises, the human might be so startled and mentally consumed that they lack a clear-cut mind to be able to turn over the driving to the AI.

- *An active system like the smoke alarm is constantly detecting the environment and ready to go off as soon as the conditions occur that will activate the alarm*

With this approach, the AI is ready to step into the driving task and will do so whenever it deems necessary. This can be handy since the human driver might not realize an emergency is arising, or might realize it but not invoke the AI to help, or be perhaps incapacitated in some manner and wanting to invoke the AI but cannot.

Downside here is that the AI might shock or startle the human driver by summarily taking over the driving and catching the human driver off-guard. If so, the human driver might try to take some dramatic action that counters the actions of the AI.

We might also end-up with the human driver become on-edge that at any moment the AI is going to take over. This might cause the human driver to get suspicious of the AI.

It could be that the AI only alerts the human driver and lets the human driver decide what the human driver wants to do. Or, it could be that the AI grabs control of the car.

- *Some system elements are intended to simply alert the human and it is then up to the human to take some form of action*

In this case, if the AI is acting as an alert, the question arises as to how best communicate the alert. If the AI rings a bell or turns on a red light, the human driver won't especially know what the declared emergency is about. Thus, the human driver might react to the "wrong" emergency in terms of what the human perceives versus what the AI detected.

If the AI tries to explain the nature of the emergency, this can use up precious time. When an emergency is arising, the odds are that there is little available time to try and explain what to do.

I am reminded that at one point my teenage novice driver children were about to potentially hit a bicyclist and I was tongue tied trying to explain the situation. I could just say "swerve to your right!" but this offered no explanation for why to do so. If I tried to say "there is a bicyclist to your left, watch out!" this provided some explanation and the desired action would be up to the driver. If I had said "there is a bicyclist to your left, swerve to your right!" it could be that the time taken to say the first part, depicting the situation, used up the available time to actually make the swerving action that would save the bike rider. Etc.

- *Some system elements such as a fire sprinkler are intended to automatically engage to save human lives and the humans being saved do not need to directly activate the life-saving effort*

This approach involves the AI taking over the driving control, which as mentioned has both pluses and minuses.

- *These emergency-only systems are intended to be used only when absolutely necessary and otherwise are silent, being somewhat out-of-sight and out-of-mind of most humans*

For emergency-only AI driving systems, they are intended only for use when an emergency driving situation arises. This begs the question though of what is considered an emergency versus not an emergency.

Also, suppose a human believes an emergency is arising but the AI has not detected it, or maybe the AI detected it and determined that it does not believe that a genuine emergency is brewing. This brings up the usual hand-off issues that arise when doing any kind of co-sharing of the driving task.

- *Such systems are not error-free in that they can at times falsely activate even when there isn't any pending emergency involved*

Some AI developers seem to think that their AI driving system is going to work perfectly and do so all of the time. This makes little sense. There is a good likelihood that the AI will have hidden bugs. There is a likelihood that the AI as devised will potentially make a wrong move. There is a chance that the AI hardware might glitch. And so on.

If an emergency-only AI system engages on a false positive, it will likely undermine confidence by the human driver that the AI is worthy to have engaged at all. There is also the concern that if the AI gets caught in a false negative and does not take action when needed, this too is worrisome since the human would assert that they relied upon the AI to deal with the emergency, but it failed in its duty to perform.

- *Humans can undermine these emergency-only systems by not abiding by them or taking other actions that reduce the effectiveness of the system*

With the co-sharing of the driving task, there is the inherent concern that you have two drivers trying to each drive the car as they see fit.

Imagine that when my children were learning to drive if I had a second set of driving controls. The odds are that I would have kept my foot on the brake nearly all of the time and been keeping a steady grip on the steering wheel. This though would have undermined their driving effort and created confusion as to which of us was really driving the car. The same can be said of the AI emergency-only driving versus the human driving.

- *Humans will at times distrust an emergency-only system and believe that the system is falsely reporting an emergency and therefore not take prescribed action*

Would we lockout the driving controls for the human whenever the AI takes over control due to a perceived emergency situation by the AI detection? This would prevent having the human driver fight with the AI in terms of what driving action to take. But the human driver is likely to have qualms about this. Suppose the AI has taken over when there wasn't a genuine emergency.

We might assume or hope that the AI in the case of acting on a false alarm (false positive) would not get the car into harm's way. This though is not necessarily the case.

Suppose the AI perceived that the car was potentially going to hit a bicyclist, and so the AI swerved the car to avoid the bike rider. Meanwhile, by swerving the car, another car in the next lane got unnerved and the driver in that car reacted by slamming on their brakes.

Meanwhile, by slamming on their brakes, the car behind them slammed into the car that had hit its brakes. All of this being precipitated by the AI that opted to avoid hitting the bicyclist.

Imagine though that the bicyclist took a quick turn away from the car and thus there really wasn't an emergency per se.

Conclusion

There are going to be AI systems that are devised to work only on an emergency basis.

Astute ones will be designed to silently be detecting what is going on and be ready to step into a task when needed. We'll need though to make sure that humans know when and how the AI is going to take action. Those humans too will be imperfect and potentially forget that the AI is there or might even end-up fighting with the AI if the human believes that the AI is wrong to take action or otherwise has qualms about the AI.

We usually think of an emergency as a situation involving the need for an urgent intervention in order to avoid or mitigate the chances of injury to life, health, or property.

There is a lot of judgment that often comes to play when declaring that a situation is an emergency. When an automated AI system tries to help out, clarity will be needed as to what constitutes an emergency and what does not.

The Hippocratic Oath states that primum non nocere, meaning first do no harm. An emergency-only AI system for a self-driving car is going to have a duty to abide by that principle, which I assure you is going to be a high burden to bear.

The emergency-only AI approach is not as easy of a path as some might at initial glance assume, and indeed for some it might even be considered insufficient, while for others it is a step forward toward the goal of a full autonomous AI self-driving car.

CHAPTER 4
ANIMAL DRAWN VEHICLES
AND
AI SELF-DRIVING CARS

CHAPTER 4

ANIMAL DRAWN VEHICLES
AND AI SELF-DRIVING CARS

I see horses. I see them most days. I'm fortunate to live nearby an equestrian center. When I drive to work in the morning there is usually someone taking a horse for a ride. The equestrian center has its own riding trails and much of the time the horses are kept inside the center's property. There are though special dirt trails that parallel the streets of my neighborhood and the horse riders can go along those paths if they wish to do so.

Living in the Los Angeles area would seem to suggest that you might rarely if ever see horses. We have lots of city environs with tall buildings and tight streets that are filled with cars and snarled with traffic. We have busy suburbs that have home after home and swimming pool after swimming pool. And yes, we do have some grassy open parks here and there and areas such as the nearby equestrian center that provide a kind of "wilderness out west" escape from the big city type of living.

When I see someone riding their horse alongside the roads in my community, I sometimes have a moment of thinking maybe I should be a cowboy and be outside steering cattle rather than working in a high-tech lab with the latest in AI systems and robotics. Sitting around a campfire at night, eating a can of beans, looking up at the vast array of star in the moonlit sky, and rustling cattle during the daylight. That's me. Well, maybe not.

71

The horse riders slowly ride their horses down the street and are wise to be cautious of the car traffic. I always try to be careful with my car when I end-up coming upon a horse and its rider, but there are some drivers here that have grown immune to the joy of seeing the horses and they drive without any consideration for these magnificent animals and their riders.

For example, the other day there was a horse rider that came up to place that the path crosses the street. The horse rider would need to come off of the path that paralleled the street and was protected by a sidewalk and slightly raised up from the road level. As the horse and rider started to go across the street, which put them directly into the path of oncoming cars, some of the car drivers seemed unimpressed that they were driving up to a horse. The horse and rider were completely vulnerable to any car driving idiot that might hit the gas and ram into them (heaven forbid!).

The car driver was driving their car as though it was just any pedestrian meandering across the street, maybe someone on a bike or walking a bike. The driver did not seem to be calculating the possibility that the horse might get riled up by a car. Inanimate objects like a bicycle are not likely to suddenly react to the presence of a car. A horse is a horse. It's an animal. If a car gets too close to some horses, and the car appears to be moving in a threatening manner (from the perspective of the horse, whether rightfully or wrongly so believing), the horse is bound to do something to indicate its concern or displeasure. I've seen some horses that came to a complete standstill. I've seen other horses that try to bolt across the street and escape the situation.

For those horses that have lived here a while, they seem quite experienced in dealing with cars. As such, these savvy horses seem to take the whole matter of being next to cars as something mundane and not especially noteworthy. Newer horses appear to not yet have reconciled the idea that they will be ridden within a few feet of moving cars. That being said, I'd assert though that even the most mature horse is going to find it objectionable if a car appears to be moving too fast and might ram into them.

The horse rider of course has a lot to do in this equation of the car and horse interaction.

Sometimes the horses are being ridden by a novice horse rider, such as a child. The child often does not yet know how to control a horse, and particularly so when the horse is riled-up. I've seen many times an unsuspecting child riding a horse that had no problems while riding the horse in the forested area of the equestrian center and believes they can well handle a horse, and then the child discovers to their dismay that it's a different story when taking the horse into the neighborhood among frantic cars, barking dogs, wild bicyclists, noisy motorcyclists, and all sorts of other people and things that the horse would not encounter in the protected forest area.

To clarify, these are not wild horses. They are domesticated horses. By-and-large, they have been trained to cope with the vagaries of our urban world. Some of them here are used for more than solely providing a ride for humans. There are some horses that are also used as so-called working animals. I'd like to emphasize that I consider any horse that is providing a ride to a person and for which the equestrian center is getting paid by the human rider, I'd call that a "working" horse in my book (it is working and earning money for someone).

Usually a working horse is one that you'd consider a beast of burden, one that has a harness and is used to pull something like a carriage or a wagon. We have an annual parade on the 4th of July and some of the horses are used to pull stagecoaches and parade floats. The crowds lining the lengthy parade route are apt to burst into applause and make ooh and ah sounds whenever the horses come along in the parade.

If you've ever been to New York City (NYC), you've likely seen the horse drawn carriages near Central Park. Tourists delight in going for a ride in the carriages and having a romantic trip. There is ongoing controversy about the horse drawn carriages and there are some that believe it is inhumane or improper to have the horses do this task, especially in the NYC environment.

Besides the romantic notion we humans have about the matter, the reality is that the horses are nearby the crazy car traffic that permeates the streets of the city that never sleeps.

According to published reports and a catalog of incidents kept by PETA, earlier this year there was a case of a horse and carriage that took off into the streets of NYC without the carriage driver, and the horse ran into two parked cars, injuring the horse and the cars. Even worse was an incident in which a horse was being raced to the front of the hack line by a carriage driver (the hack line is where the carriages wait to find someone willing to pay for a ride, like waiting for a cab), and the entire carriage overturned and injured the horse.

I don't want to seem to only be picking on my East Coast NYC friends, and so it is noteworthy that there have been incidents in other locations that allow horse drawn carriages too. For example, last year there was an incident in St. Louis, Missouri that involved a horse drawing a carriage that ran into a moving car. In Durango, Colorado, a driver left his carriage unattended and the horse took off and ran randomly in the streets. Charleston, South Carolina had an incident last year in which a horse and carriage ran into a moving car. And so on.

One of the most famous recent incidents did take place in NYC. A few years ago, a horse named Goldie broke free of the harness and galloped for eleven blocks in the streets of NYC. I know that New Yorkers are used to seeing unusual and at times strange antics on their streets, though I'd bet that a horse galloping on its own would be something that even the hardened New Yorkers would stop for a moment to see. Can you take a selfie of a galloping horse behind you while standing on 5th Avenue and post it to social media and get lots of views? I'm sure you can.

There are some people that rely upon a horse and buggy as their primary form of transportation. In Lancaster County, the Amish routinely use a multitude of horse and buggy wagons to get around. There is a false assumption that the Amish are prevented by their religious beliefs in riding in a car, but this is not the case. They aren't supposed own a car. They can ride in a car, if the situation arises.

Generally, they use a horse and buggy to get around in their locale. This is sufficient for their living purposes.

Those of us in the United States might not realize there are many places in the world that still rely upon horses, mules, donkeys, and other draft animals as a crucial part of their living. Believe it or not, the cost of having a draft animal, including its upkeep, and the lesser need to have things such as gas stations and auto mechanic shops, makes it sensible to use beasts of burden in some parts of today's world. The use of horse drawn carriages in NYC and other places is marginally a necessity, one might argue, while places that rely upon draft animals to farm and otherwise make a living are arguably more dependent upon such matters.

I'd perhaps be remiss if I left out camels. They too are a beast of burden. They are used in places in the world that can have them come in contact with cars by having the camels walk in car traffic, frequently so. Dogs can be beasts of burden too. Think about dog sleds. A dog sled can be driven onto roads that also have car traffic.

One concern about having these animals in car traffic situations involves the rather obvious point that the animal can get injured or killed by cars. Likewise, such an animal could ram into or run over a car, potentially injuring occupants in the car. We need to also consider the health hazard overall to a draft animal that when in traffic might be breathing in the harmful exhaust and fumes of the cars. This can add-up over time, the more that the draft animal goes into traffic.

It can be tricky and frightening to a draft animal to be amongst moving cars. This causes emotional stress for the animal. There is rather apparent physical stresses too due to the continual walking or running on a paved street, which is bound to be abrasive to their legs and feet or hoofs. One of the complaints lobbed at the horse and carriage trade here in the United States is that the horses eventually end-up with leg problems as a result of so much walking on the hard surfaces of asphalt streets.

For most of us, we probably in our daily driving routine rarely encounter any draft animals that are pulling a wagon or buggy or carriage and doing so in or close to the car traffic. In my case, I'd need to drive to a ranch here in Southern California to likely have such contact with me and my car. Nonetheless, there is a chance that at some point you'll be driving in your car and come upon an animal drawn vehicle. For some people, maybe this happens each day, while for others it perhaps happens in a blue moon.

Either way, it is expected that a human driver of a car be ready and able to properly and appropriately drive when near to an animal drawn vehicle. This is covered in most states as part of the rules embodied in their approved official driving rules. For California, the Department of Motor Vehicles (DMV) provides an indication of the do's and don'ts when you are driving nearby animal drawn vehicles. Besides wanting to encourage safe driving in such settings, the human driver can also be ticketed and suffer various driving penalties if they drive adversely, unsafely, or in an illegal manner when driving nearby to animal drawn vehicles. It's the code, live with it!

What does this have to do with AI self-driving cars?

At the Cybernetic AI Self-Driving Car Institute, we are developing AI software for self-driving cars. One aspect involves the AI system being able to cope with driving when nearby animal drawn vehicles.

This is generally considered an edge or corner case, rightfully so due to its rarity in the everyday city or suburb driving situations, but nonetheless it is a legal requirement that human drivers must be aware of and obey the rules and in our view so should an AI self-driving car.

You can't just wave your hands as an AI developer and complain that encountering an animal drawn vehicle is an obscure use case.

Obscure or not, the AI had better drive properly, otherwise the animal(s) might be endangered, any human riders or drivers of an animal drawn carriage might be endangered by a car, and even the car itself and its occupants could be endangered (plus nearby pedestrians or other humans that could be involved in a potential car crash or incident sparked by the interaction of the car and the draft animal).

I'd like to first clarify and introduce the notion that there are varying levels of AI self-driving cars. The topmost level is considered Level 5. A Level 5 self-driving car is one that is being driven by the AI and there is no human driver involved. For the design of Level 5 self-driving cars, the auto makers are even removing the gas pedal, brake pedal, and steering wheel, since those are contraptions used by human drivers. The Level 5 self-driving car is not being driven by a human and nor is there an expectation that a human driver will be present in the self-driving car. It's all on the shoulders of the AI to drive the car.

For self-driving cars less than a Level 5, there must be a human driver present in the car. The human driver is currently considered the responsible party for the acts of the car. The AI and the human driver are co-sharing the driving task. In spite of this co-sharing, the human is supposed to remain fully immersed into the driving task and be ready at all times to perform the driving task. I've repeatedly warned about the dangers of this co-sharing arrangement and predicted it will produce many untoward results.

Let's focus herein on the true Level 5 self-driving car. Much of the comments apply to the less than Level 5 self-driving cars too, but the fully autonomous AI self-driving car will receive the most attention in this discussion.

Here's the usual steps involved in the AI driving task:

- Sensor data collection and interpretation
- Sensor fusion
- Virtual world model updating
- AI action planning
- Car controls command issuance

Another key aspect of AI self-driving cars is that they will be driving on our roadways in the midst of human driven cars too. There are some pundits of AI self-driving cars that continually refer to a utopian world in which there are only AI self-driving cars on the public roads. Currently there are about 250+ million conventional cars in the United States alone, and those cars are not going to magically disappear or become true Level 5 AI self-driving cars overnight.

Indeed, the use of human driven cars will last for many years, likely many decades, and the advent of AI self-driving cars will occur while there are still human driven cars on the roads. This is a crucial point since this means that the AI of self-driving cars needs to be able to contend with not just other AI self-driving cars, but also contend with human driven cars. It is easy to envision a simplistic and rather unrealistic world in which all AI self-driving cars are politely interacting with each other and being civil about roadway interactions. That's not what is going to be happening for the foreseeable future. AI self-driving cars and human driven cars will need to be able to cope with each other.

Returning to the matter of driving a car when nearby to animal drawn vehicles, let's consider the kinds of driving tactics and strategies that an AI system for a self-driving car should be imbued with in order to safely deal with such situations.

I'm sure there are some AI developers that would immediately claim that the AI does not need any special capability for driving when nearby animal drawn vehicles. They would contend that if an AI system can navigate and drive a car on everyday streets, it would presumably be able to drive when nearby animal drawn vehicles. Indeed, they would assert that there is nothing unsual or special to be done, and the AI can consider an animal drawn vehicle to be no different than any other moving vehicle on the road.

Hogwash.

This kind of thinking is going to get AI self-driving cars into some bad predicaments that could have otherwise been more safely handled.

If we just play the game that an animal drawn vehicle is no different than any other moving vehicle, the odds are that eventually and inevitably something will go awry. For those pundits that are strong advocates of AI self-driving cars, I assure you that the day that an AI self-driving car gets entangled in an adverse situation with an animal driven vehicle, and especially if there is any injury to humans or animals, it will become a rallying cry for those that say AI self-driving cars are not ready for being on our roads.

An AI developer that shrugs off the possibility is missing a bigger picture. An AI self-driving car pundit that is vocally supportive of AI self-driving cars will find that even one such adverse incident can undermine months or possibly even years of potential public-trust that might have been built up for AI self-driving cars. AI self-driving car maims horse. AI self-driving car crashes into horse drawn carriage. Horses scared by AI self-driving car and sprint away, fearing for their lives. These are all headlines that can catch like wildfire and then damage the image of AI self-driving cars, which will be very hard to undo or overcome.

Let's consider what the AI should be doing regarding animal drawn vehicles.

First, the detection of an animal drawn vehicle is key to being able to undertake any potential actions about it. The sensors of the AI self-driving car need to try and ascertain whether an animal drawn vehicle is nearby. This might be harder to do than you think.

For humans, we readily can look around the surroundings of a car and be able to discern that there is say a horse over there and it is pulling a carriage. Easy to do. For most AI systems, this is a much harder task. Generally, the AI will make use of cameras to visually examine the surroundings of the car. Pictures or video are then analyzed by software routines that are often trained to find everyday objects in a street scene, such as other cars, buses, bicyclists, pedestrians, and the like.

Using Machine Learning (ML) and Deep Learning (DL), the visual images are assessed and interpreted by Artificial Neural Networks (ANN's or sometimes referred to as simply NN's). These ML/DL elements were likely trained via thousands upon thousands of images of everyday street scenes, of which, there were visual aspects or clues that could lend toward identifying what is in the image. As a result of this training, the AI is supposed to be able to discern what kinds of objects are nearby and also associate those objects with potential behaviors.

One issue about these ANN's is that the training set of data needs to encompass a wide enough range of images that the training will provide sufficient examples for dealing with the real world. Suppose we fed thousands of street scene images into a ML/DL and purposely did not include scenes that had light posts and nor fire hydrants. The ANN doesn't somehow magically realize that the images don't contain something. Instead, it trains based on what is presented to it.

Without any training on the recognizing of light posts and fire hydrants, this means that in the real-world the AI self-driving car is not going to be informed when a light post or fire hydrant is nearby. I'd wager that most of us notice fire hydrants when we are trying to park our cars, being wary of parking near to one for concern of getting a ticket. Imagine if you did not even know what a fire hydrant looked like, which therefore you would likely park next to one, innocently, unknowingly, since you would just assume the thing sitting there was some kind of inconsequential object, a blob as it were.

I mention all of this because the same notion can be applied to an animal drawn vehicle. If the image processing portion of the AI system has not be explicitly trained or programmed to recognize animal drawn vehicles, there will be no specific means for the AI to recognize that one is nearby. Instead, there will be an unknown blob. The AI will at least potentially realize that something is there, and in addition to the visual images there will likely be radar, ultrasonic, and LIDAR that will detect the presence of the thing.

Unfortunately, detecting the presence of something is not enough, since you also would be better off knowing what the thing actually is. Categorized as a blob, the AI really cannot do much in terms of anticipating what the blob might do. Is it stationary and unlikely to move? If a horse drawn carriage is sitting at the curb and waiting to take on passengers, it is momentarily still, but soon enough it will start to move into traffic. Not knowing that the unknown object is a horse drawn carriage, the AI might assume that the stationary object is always unmoving and perhaps permanently stationed in the spot that it resides.

Detection then is crucial for the AI to be able to deal with animal drawn vehicles. There must be ML/DL that was undertaken specifically to include animal drawn vehicles. The nature and types of animal drawn vehicles would need to have been varied enough to allow for the real-world variety of circumstances that the AI self-driving car might itself in.

This brings up another aspect about AI self-driving cars, namely their being internationally ready. Much of the work on AI self-driving car is taking place currently in the United States. There is an inherent bias on the part of the AI developers to concentrate on the kinds of roads and roadway situations encountered in the United States. That's fine and makes sense for aiming at AI self-driving cars that will work well in the United States, but it also provides the potential downside that the AI self-driving cars won't do well in other countries, being unable to contend with the international differences.

If you are an auto maker or tech firm and mainly care about the U.S. market, you are doing just fine to have a U.S.-only mindset. On the other hand, if you want to ultimately have your AI self-driving cars be able to work properly in Europe, and in Asia, and in all other parts of the world, you need to be considering how to establish the groundwork in your AI system to be able to deal with those other locales. If you've ever developed software for a global market, you know that you need to build into your software a multi-lingual capability and also that it needs to be culturally appropriate as to the cultures that will use the software.

In the case of an AI self-driving car, the nature of the differences between the U.S. and other countries can be quite dramatic in terms of the driving task and the driving scenes. One such difference is going to be the animal drawn vehicles aspects. As mentioned earlier, it is likely rare in the U.S. for an AI self-driving car to come upon animal drawn vehicles, while in certain other countries it would be considered commonplace.

Besides the AI self-driving car being able to detect directly whether or not an animal drawn vehicle is nearby, the AI might also be tipped to the possibility by a passenger in the AI self-driving car. People that are riding in an AI self-driving car are likely going to want to carry on a dialogue with the AI system. Some AI developers only believe that the passengers will give a direction such as take me to the ballgame, and no other conversation will occur. This is narrow thinking and the reality is that people will want to interact with the AI, in the same fashion that they might interact with a human cab driver or a chauffeur.

As such, a human occupant might try to tell the AI that there is a horse drawn carriage over to the right of the road and the carriage waiting to proceed into traffic.

Perhaps the AI self-driving car is in New York City. The human inside the self-driving car is concerned that the AI of the self-driving might not have detected the horse carriage and be worried that the AI is not going to take appropriate precautions. The concerned passenger of the self-driving car might then bring up the matter to alert the AI. Hopefully, the AI would have already detected the presence of the horse and the carriage and reassure the human occupant that the AI realizes the matter and will be taking appropriate precautions.

Another means for the AI to potentially be aware of the presence of the animal drawn vehicle might be due to V2V (vehicle-to-vehicle) electronic communications. Suppose that another AI self-driving car is a block ahead of your AI self-driving car. The AI of that self-driving car detects the presence of a horse drawn carriage.

The AI might then broadcast out via V2V to other nearby AI self-driving cars that there is an animal drawn vehicle on the street and thus forewarn those other AI self-driving cars.

This same kind of electronic heads-up could come via V2I (vehicle-to-infrastructure) and possibly via V2P (vehicle-to-pedestrian) communications.

Suppose that NYC decides to put up computers at various street corners to be able to aid in monitoring traffic, and perhaps one aspect involves those devices being aware of horse drawn carriages. Imagine that the traffic signals are controlled by those computing devices and purposely go quickly to a green light whenever a horse drawn carriage approaches the intersection. This might be a safety technique implemented to reduce the amount of time that the horse drawn carriages have to sit idle while waiting for a green light (I suppose tourists riding in the carriage would like the green lights too).

The NYC transportation department might setup computers at the street corners and include the use of V2I to broadcast out a warning, such as whenever there is an animal drawn vehicle at the corner. The AI self-driving cars that are equipped with V2I would then be forewarned about the presence of the horse drawn carriage.

In a similar manner, there are some that are envisioning that pedestrians will also be able to communicate with AI self-driving cars, doing so via electronic means referred to as V2P. It could be that a pedestrian, upon seeing a horse drawn carriage coming down 8th Street, might use their smart watch to send out a signal to then let nearby AI self-driving cars know that the animal drawn vehicle is there.

The detection of the animal drawn vehicle is the first part of the driving task for the AI system. The next step involves updating the virtual world model being used by the AI system.

This is an internal kind of model that indicates where various objects are, as related to the position of the self-driving car, and also indicates the movement and direction of those objects. You might think of this as a kind of air traffic control capability, trying to monitor traffic and where it is and where it might be headed.

The really difficult part comes once the AI action planning component analyzes the virtual world model and determine what kinds of next driving actions are appropriate.

Animals can do wild things.

Of course, yes, I realize that humans can do wild things too. A human driving a car can wildly opt to veer across lanes or go head-on towards other cars. It happens. Generally, we live in a world whereby our usual expectation is that other human drivers are going to do rational things and drive relatively safely. If that were not the case, I assure you that we would have many more car accidents and traffic related deaths than we do today. It is a kind of miracle that each day we have millions upon millions of cars being driven on our roadways and we are not inundated in nonstop chaos and destruction. A miracle, I say!

Anyway, without offending any animal lovers, I hope we can agree that there is a chance that animals can do wild things too. The AI needs to be anticipating what the animal drawn vehicle might be doing and where and how it will be going next.

The animal drawn vehicle is most likely being driven by a human. In theory, the human driver is directing the animal. The animal is merely pulling the vehicle and not deciding where to go, nor deciding when to stop, when to turn, etc.

Consider that we might have a situation whereby the carriage driver is fighting with the animal drawing the carriage. It might be a horse that refuses to proceed ahead. Maybe the horse is reluctant to make a turn at the corner. Perhaps the horse has come to a halt in the middle of the street, either because it fears getting hit by a car or maybe just because it wants to come to a stop.

The point being that an animal might overtake the efforts of the driver of the animal drawn vehicle. The AI cannot assume that the human driver of the animal drawn vehicle will do the right thing in terms of directing the vehicle, and also that the human driver might want to do the right thing but be prevented or inhibited by the animal drawing the vehicle.

There is also the case of the animal drawn vehicle that has no human driver involved. This is rare and presumably only in cases wherein the human driver has perhaps failed to get into the carriage and let it loose, or maybe fallen out of the carriage, or fainted while in the carriage, etc.

The AI needs to be wary of the animal drawn carriage. It would be safest to provide as much leeway as possible, having the AI action plan targeting a sufficiently wide berth to the animal drawn carriage. Predicting the path of where the animal drawn carriage might go can be tricky. There should be multiple potential paths plotted, under the assumption that the animal might opt to go in some otherwise unsuspecting direction or the carriage driver might do so.

The AI should try to avoid any sudden moves of the car. A quick acceleration or a sudden change of lanes can be alarming to the animal (and likely to the driver of the animal drawn vehicle).

Using the horn of the self-driving car would be generally ill-advised when around an animal drawn carriage.

My mentioning the horn on an AI self-driving car might seem peculiar to you. What, the AI can use a horn?

AI self-driving car can in theory make use of its horn, which we all likely would hope might be done rather judiciously. Some AI developers have insisted that the AI should never use the horn at all. I think that's a bit of an overkill and assert that having a horn and using it can be handy in certain circumstances. I'm not advocating that an AI self-driving car should be incessantly honking its horn and trying to draw attention or provoke other drivers. The horn should be used only when appropriate.

I refer to this as the conspicuity of an AI self-driving car, which means there are times at which it will make a lot of sense for the AI self-driving car to be conspicuous.

The AI self-driving car should consider the animal drawn vehicle to be capable of the same kinds of maneuvers that a car might be able to make. The speed of the animal drawn vehicle is likely to be less than that of a speeding car, though a team of horses can get going pretty fast if they want to do so. In any case, the AI self-driving car should plan on going slowly when near to the animal drawn vehicle. Plus, it should have a ready-made escape plan, in case the animal drawn vehicle suddenly goes awry.

Conclusion

For most of us, an animal drawn vehicle is something quaint. We see them at tourist areas such as in NYC near Central Park. We might see them at parades. They might be seen at farms or ranches. In some parts of the world, animal drawn vehicles are a customary practice. They are continually in and around car traffic. That's a fact of life in those areas.

An AI self-driving car needs to be prepared to cope with situations involving animal drawn vehicles.

Treating an animal drawn vehicle as merely some kind of large-size unidentifiable blob that seems to be on the roadway is insufficient.

The odds are that there will be ugly and untoward entanglements between naïve and ill-prepared AI self-driving cars and the real-world animal drawn vehicles that might be encountered.

We'd all prefer savvy AI self-driving cars that are ready and able to contend with animal driven vehicles. The horses, donkeys, mules, dogs, camels, and other beasts of burden will be thankful that the AI developers considered how to best assist and be compatible with those working animals. Let's all work on that!

CHAPTER 5

CHESS PLAY
AND
AI SELF-DRIVING CARS

CHAPTER 5

CHESS PLAY
AND AI SELF-DRIVING CARS

The bishop took the opposing knight and the game was in check.

The other player assessed their situation and realized that the matter was now hopeless. Begrudgingly, the player conceded defeat and walked away from the board, vowing to never make the same mistake again. The winner was somewhat relieved because though it had looked promising that a win was within grasp, there were still a number of available counter-moves that the opponent could have used to try and gain momentum towards a possible win. Having the opponent concede or resign the game seemed maybe premature and almost surprising, perhaps even objectionable (hey, keep trying!), and yet there was no reason to not accept the concession since a win is a win.

What am I talking about?

For those of you familiar with chess, you likely recognize that I've described a rather typical end-game of a chess match.

If you are interested in AI, you likely would want to know about chess since the game has been used to help derive many of the AI techniques that we use today for all kinds of other endeavors. Chess is a deceptively easy game because the nature of the rules are relatively simple and readily described, and yet playing games successfully can be quite challenging (when I say successfully, I mean winning at chess).

Humans have been competing against each other since perhaps the Middle Ages to see who can be the best at chess.

It has always been hoped that we might be able to figure out how humans play chess so that we could then improve how humans can further play chess. Suppose that humans are able to play chess to a certain degree of sophistication, meaning being able to win against other humans a particular percentage of the time. Let's study the topmost players and see if by doing so we are able to discover how they are so accomplished. We then share their tactics and strategies with other humans that perhaps are able to build upon that foundation and get even better at chess.

Without understanding why we make various moves during a chess match, it can be problematic to know what to do during a chess game. Is it better or worse to move a given piece on the chessboard to some other spot on the chessboard at any given time in a particular state of the chess game? No one can say for sure in all instances of any permutation, and we continually are seeking to find out to some approximate degree what are good moves versus bad moves for any state of the game.

If I only tell you the rules of the game, I'm not particularly also indicating what kinds of tactics and strategies to employ. You might gradually figure out on your own the kinds of winning tactics and strategies, but presumably it might help you if I gave you a head-start by providing what are believed to be good versus bad tactics and strategies when planning the game of chess.

Over time, we hopefully bootstrap humans toward getting better and better at playing chess. This is intended to be done by purposeful action. In other words, we are not getting better solely due to random chance and nor do perhaps only by the volume of people perchance playing the game, but instead because we've gleaned more about the good and bad ways to play chess.

One way to presumably try to gauge successful chess playing involves looking at the step-by-step play made during actual chess games. Avid chess players have been collecting game steps since nearly the origin of the game. There are books upon books listing the step-by-step moves in thousands and upon thousands of chess matches that have been played over time.

A black-box approach to analyzing how to best play chess can be undertaken by studying those step-by-step listed games. In that manner, you really don't know anything about what is happening in the person's head, and all you have to go with is the result of their chess moves. Why did I start a chess game with a move of my pawn? By studying the list of moves, you really don't know why I did what I did, and the only thing you can do is see that I did so. From that listing, you can try to guess at what I might have been thinking.

Suppose you guess that I moved my pawn because I thought that the pawn should be in the middle of the chessboard. You now have a derived tactic, namely, assuming that I'm a really good chess player, you infer that by having a pawn at the middle of the chessboard it is a wise move and will ultimately increase the chances of winning a chess match. If I was a lousy chess player, you'd not be so enamored of my pawn move and likely assume I did something either by random chance or had dumb luck.

Maybe you decide to not only try and derive what I was thinking, doing so by looking just at the results or data listing of the steps performed in a chess match, but you also opt to ask me why I made that move of the pawn. This will allow you to take the black-box approach and see if you can poke into the head of the chess player, perhaps becoming a white box or transparent one.

You ask me directly why I did the move. I tell you that I did so because I was actually trying to free up potential movement for my knight and the pawn was in the way, so I moved it into the middle of the chessboard.

Well, that's interesting. The earlier black-box data-only derived tactic was that a pawn should be in the middle of the chessboard. The tactic I claimed that I was using involved moving the pawn not per se for the sake of the pawn, instead it was done to provide an avenue or path to use another one of my chess pieces, my knight. You might therefore opt to rescind the derived tactic, crossing out the notion that the pawn should be in the middle of the chessboard as an overarching tactic or strategy, and you replace it with the approach that the knight needs room to move.

Here's a question for you: Did I really in fact intentionally and with my mental thinking faculties come to the choice of moving the pawn to open up space for the knight, or did I just say that to try and justify my move?

Neither you or me really can know what occurred in my brain that led to the moving of the pawn. Maybe I moved the pawn because it was Thursday and there was going to be a full moon that night, which is to say that there might be any number of explanations for why I *really* made the move of the pawn. My telling you one particular explanation is not necessarily what really happened in my head. I have no way to know what really happened, and nor do you.

Note that I am not suggesting that I was maybe lying to you about why I believed that I moved the pawn. It is genuinely possible that I have a belief that I moved the pawn for the reason I articulated. Can I somehow inspect my own neurons in my brain and be able to physically and biologically explain how those neurons and the brain functioned to make that actual choice? Nope. Can't do it.

The point being that to better play chess we only have the ability to analyze the results of chess matches and try to derive from that data what seem to be good tactics and strategies, which we can couple with those rationalizations or explanations that chess players claim they did and that are presumably good chess playing tactics and strategies. None of that reveals the true inner workings of our brain and what our minds were doing. We instead have reasonings that offer seemingly logical explanations for the chess playing behavior.

Some might say that you don't need to know what actually happened in a chess players brain. The results of the games and the explanations by the chess players is sufficient, they contend.

Others though are worried that the logic-based approach to ascertaining chess play might not be sufficient. If we could unlock the secrets of the brain and figure out how it really plays chess, we might then not only be able to get better at chess, it might also give us greater insight into the brain and how we think. If we can decode how we think, this could allow us to improve our thinking overall, about all kinds of things, far beyond chess itself.

Chess as a Path to Thinking and AI

Understanding chess playing is more than merely being able to play chess.

Some hope that if we can better understand chess play, this can allow us to get better at all kinds of games, and furthermore get better at all kinds of thinking and the solving of problems of all kinds. Maybe we can use chess to act as a kind of Rosetta Stone to figure out how humans really think. Chess becomes a convenient tool to aid in decoding the mysteries of the human mind and how it works. Chess is incidental to the larger macroscopic picture of aiming at illuminating the basic foundation of human thought.

I mention this aspect about chess as a possible key to unlocking human thinking due to the often repeated comment that chess is only a game, and why are we spending so much time on some silly game? It could be that we spend all this time and attention on studying of chess play, and all we end-up with is that we are better at playing chess. How does that help world hunger? How does that aid solving real-world problems?

The hope is that the more we understand chess, the more we understand how we think.

Yes, admittedly, chess is only a game. It takes place in a constrained set of rules and does not especially rise to the nature of our open-ended and more challenging aspects we face as a society and in the real-world. Chess is interesting, it is fun, it is considered by many to be a sport. Besides those elements it also offers the possibility of getting inside of our heads.

There's another angle too on chess, namely the desire to create artificially intelligent systems, and for which maybe chess will help us to get there.

If we can create an AI system that plays chess well, presumably we might discover how humans think and be able to embody that into machines. Once again, we would be using chess as a means to an end, wherein the end-game is to be able to create AI systems. The fact that we might have done so by also being able to create really good chess playing AI is not as consequential as the notion that by doing so we elevate the capabilities of AI overall.

I would dare say that from the perspective of achieving true AI, for me, I don't care if it is chess or Monopoly or tidily winks, meaning that whatever "game" might be the provocateur that enables us to reach true AI, I'm generally for it. Allow me to say that I do enjoy chess (which I mention herein so that I won't get bombarded with hate mail from chess lovers), and I hope that chess is one avenue toward getting to true AI, preferably a strong avenue that offers foreseeable and motivating and earnest promise, but I am not so wedded to chess that I would want it to be do-or-die, namely we put all our table stakes on chess being the miraculous unlocking puzzle piece. Let's not do that.

One difficulty though is that we might be able to make machines play really well at chess, even being able to best humans, and yet this might not necessarily mean that we are getting closer to understanding how humans think and nor that the machine embodies that capability.

I offer that caution because the latest AI systems to play chess are continually being touted as "superhuman" – a phrase that I find disconcerting. When you refer to an AI system in terminology that says it is superhuman, I'm concerned that many people assume you are suggesting that the AI system does what humans do, namely thinking, and do it even better.

Let's be clear about things and all agree that the manner in which the "superhuman" AI playing chess systems operate is not necessarily how humans think.

Imagine that I was able to create a mechanical arm that had gears and wires. At first, it could not lift as heavy a weight as a human can. Let's say it is considered sub-human at that juncture of development. I keep working on it and finally I get it to lift heavier weights than a human. I have invented a "superhuman" arm. It is in fact stronger than any human arm!

Have I therefore been able to recreate in a machine the same thing as a human arm? I don't think so.

It would seem that any reasonable person would agree that I have created a really good mechanical arm, but it is not the same as a human arm. In an equivalent means, I am suggesting that though we might at this time have so-called "superhuman" AI systems that can play chess better than a human chess player, we are making a stretch to suggest that it means the AI system is able to think like a human.

We might have simply found some means to arrive at "thinking" in a completely different way than the actual way in which the human mind works.

I suppose you might argue that if we can achieve "thinking" via some other means than how the human mind works, we are doing pretty good and maybe have no need to worry whether or not it thinks as humans do. I would almost go along with that logic, but I'd like to point out that these AI chess playing systems are mainly confined to playing chess and other such games. We do not as yet know if they will "scale" to other kinds of thinking efforts. This means that it could be a false dead-end in that yes it might help us to create AI to play games, yet maybe that's all it provides us in the end. We don't yet know.

Chess as a Driving Metaphor

I often find myself mentally wandering over to the topic of chess when doing other kinds of mental activities. Perhaps you do so too.

Each morning I get onto the freeway to drive to work. I have about an hour or more commute that I drive while on the freeway. The freeway will have stretches that involve jam packed traffic, and other portions where the traffic is somewhat sparse and moving freely. This is Los Angeles traffic, notorious for its willingness to get snarled for the littlest of reasons. A car that pulls over on the freeway will attract human drivers to gaze at the car, and these gawkers then tend to slow down or otherwise trip-up traffic, often cascading into a miles long slowing and stopping of cars. Lookie loos are but one of the many reasons that we have our infamous stop-and-go traffic.

At times, I play chess games while driving. I don't mean that I have a chessboard setup in my car. Instead, I am refereeing to "chess" in a metaphorical kind of way.

We all have occasion to suggest that we are doing some task and it is a chess-like effort. When my son used to play Little League baseball, we'd sometimes describe a baseball game in terms of chess. If the opposing team puts a certain pitcher up on the mound, what is our counter-move? If we put our best batter at the top of our batting order, will we reveal too soon the batting strength that we have? These are akin to playing chess and deciding how to make use of your chess pieces.

While driving my car, I look at the traffic ahead of me on the freeway and I envision a kind of chessboard. The cars directly ahead of me are particular chess pieces. That blue sports car to my left, its like a rook, and seems to go directly forward, while that beige sedan to my right Is more like a bishop, as it has been veering into other lanes at sharp angles. That big truck can go wherever it wants to go and no one will challenge it, as such I consider it to be the queen on the chessboard at the moment. The gaps between the cars are equated to empty spaces on a chessboard.

Which car, with each being essentially a chess piece, will next occupy that open board spot to my right, and how will they get there?

And so the chess game begins. If the open spot is immediately available, I can move my car directly into the opening. Suppose though that the opening is "guarded" by other nearby cars. I can potentially get to that open spot by first pulling ahead of the car to my left and maneuvering in front of that car by getting into its lane.

I next would zip ahead of the car that had been in front of me when I was in the prior lane, being able to do so now that I'm in the lane to the left. This then positions me to potentially slide into that open slot by crossing back into my former lane and then into the lane that was earlier to my right. I'll need though to let the traffic in that targeted lane continue forward just a tad, and then time it just right to pop into that opening.

I don't expect you to have followed my convoluted description of the moves that I made to get into that momentary opening in the lane to might right. Instead, I was just trying to illustrate the kinds of chess-like moves that I mentally entertain while driving on the freeway. I had to calculate where the other "chess" pieces are (the cars and trucks around me), I had to gauge the openings available for a move, I then devised a series of tactical moves that would get me positioned to get into the desired opening.

Sometimes the chess plays are straightforward, and I can execute them without issue. In other cases, I might mentally make my plan, such as the one I've just described, and it needs to be re-planned due to the changing traffic conditions. Keeping in mind that I'm on a freeway and going maybe 50-60 miles per hour, each of these chess plays are occurring in real-time. From the moment I think up a series of moves it might be just a few seconds once I've then executed those moves.

Furthermore, the moves that I planned out might only be valid for a few momentary seconds. Suppose the car that was to my left suddenly and unexpectedly sped-up? This would ruin my plan of trying to get ahead of that driver, which was a crucial initial step in my chess moves. I'd either need to back-down from the chess plan, or maybe concoct a new series of moves. It is a kind of cat-and-mouse match, continually requiring a reassessment of the freeway (the chessboard) and what seems viable to undertake.

Timing in chess play is considered vital in most competitive matches since there is usually a certain amount of time allowed per each move. This use of a real-time timing constraint forces the human chess player to make a choice that must take into account the available time for their thinking processes to work. Though you might want to try and use your mind to explore all possible permutations and combinations, which it's not likely you could do anyway, you nonetheless must "cut short" this thinking and make a choice.

It used to be that many chess players would mail via the postal service each move to someone else they were playing against, giving the other person days or maybe even weeks to decide upon each and every move. Though some might still do this kind of slow play or snail play, the chess playing community has embraced fast play more so than slow play. One interesting question to ponder involves whether there is a material difference in chess play based on being able to play with nearly unlimited time to make a choice versus being confronted with very little time.

Most studies show that the difference between fast real-time such as just a few seconds versus longer real-time such as a few minutes tend to reveal better or worse play choices (the radically shortened time tends toward worse choices). This is tempered somewhat by the nature of the players and the moments and states of the chess match. If you have a really masterful chess player, a grandmaster, playing against a novice, it is likely that the grandmaster can make very fast choices since the chess plays are more predictable and known, plus if the grandmaster does happen to make a mistake they know it is likely readily fixable over the course of the game.

Top chess players when going head-to-head will play very fast during portions of the game that they've all come to know as predictable and will slow down once they hit the portion of the game that is in less predictable territory. For example, the opening of chess has been so exhaustively studied and the number of sensible moves is low enough that it can be very quick at the start of a chess match for players that know what they are doing. The same kind of super-fast moves can occur toward the end of the chess match, which often involves having very few chess pieces left on the board and therefore the number of variants of moves is lessened (along with their being many known end-game moves that you can employ).

The middlegame is often the portion that takes the most time for chess players to grapple with. You've gotten past the known opening gambits, and you are not yet to a point of thinning out the chessboard to be at the end-game. If you watch chess players during the middlegame, including even the grandmasters, you will often see them put their hands to their heads and they seem to go into a deep-thinking trance. We cannot know for sure what is happening in their noggins, but presumably they are having to consider moves on a rawer basis, going beyond the predictable patterns they've seen many times before for the opening and ending of the chess match. Depending upon what the middlegame board positions are, it can be unfamiliar territory as to the landscape and require more apt attention.

In the case of my doing a kind of mental chess when I am driving my car, I am equally faced with a real-time chess match. For each instance of deciding what my next driving move will be, I am doing so perhaps every 5 to 10 seconds of time. This turns out to be around 300 or so "moves" during my hour or so commute. If any particular move is poorly planned or poorly executed, it means that I've not proceeded in my commute in as presumably a timely manner as I might have hoped.

That topic brings up something that is perhaps not quite the equivalent of normal chess play. In chess, you finish a chess game as either a winner, a loser, or with a draw. The goal is to essentially capture the king of the other player. If you can do so, you are the winner. If the other player can capture your king first, you are the loser. If neither of you seem to be able to capture the other player's king, it is considered a draw (there are other variants on how the win, lose, or draw can occur).

When I am driving my car and using a chess metaphor, there isn't quite an overall win, lose, or draw that happens to be the end-goal. Usually, I am desirous of getting to work in the fastest way that also includes being safe. In that sense, you could suggest that a win is when I get to work at a shortest feasible time and do so without having gotten into a car accident. Each move must encompass the risks involved in safely driving the car. The overall safety of the driving journey is paramount and would usually be considered a much higher priority than the timing of getting to work.

If I make a wrong move in my driving chess game, it could either delay my driving time, or worse it could involve a car accident. There is a potential life-or-death kind of calculation immersed in this pretend chess. When playing chess at a chessboard, you normally aren't worried about a life-or-death consequence (other than maybe in a James Bond movie). The stakes might be high when playing an actual chess game, perhaps prestige or money is on the line, but rarely does it have death or bodily injury at stake.

I've spoken to police officers and ambulance drivers that must at times drive for emergency purposes and therefore drive at high speeds in everyday traffic. For them, this idea of conducting a chess match in driving is heightened because they have true life-or-death stakes involved. Even though their sirens are blaring, and their blinking lights are trying to get the attention of everyday drivers, it is still a high risk action to drive very fast and opt to go through red lights or take other dire driving actions.

The chances of them hitting another car is increased and the chances of another car ramming into them is increased. They are taking such risks because there is the presumed risk involved of someone perhaps dying if they do not get to their destination fast enough (bless their hearts for taking such risks!). As a society, we seem to accept such risks, which I'll point out are not only risks to the police officer driving the police car or the ambulance driver of the fire fighter driver, but there are obviously heightened risks to the everyday driver. The everyday driver is absorbing some of that risk since they could get hit by the emergency responding driver or they could inadvertently ram into the emergency responding driver.

Back to my driving with my chess metaphor in mind, I consider the freeway to be a continually moving chessboard. From my perspective, while driving along at sometimes 60 miles per hour or going in snarled traffic at 6 miles per hour, I imagine that the chessboard radiates out from my car. My car is the cornerstone for the imaginary chessboard. The distance ahead that I can see is the front far edge of my chessboard. The distance behind me that I can see via my rearview mirror is the rear far edge of my chessboard.

A normal chessboard is 8 rows and 8 columns consisting of a square board containing 64 spots. For my car driving, I consider each car length to be the equivalent of a spot. In terms of however many cars ahead that I can see, it is the number of spots for my metaphorical chessboard for that moment in time at the front of my car. Likewise, the same is said about the chessboard spots behind me. The chessboard is a rectangle that normally has just a few spots in width, such as maybe I am on a four-lane freeway and so the chessboard is four spots or squares wide.

When the freeway roadway is flat and I can see ahead quite a bit, I might have 10 to 20 car lengths ahead that I can see, and maybe 5-10 car lengths behind me that I can see. Therefore, my mental chessboard is perhaps 15 to 30 rows in total and let's say by 4 columns wide in size. This won't last very long though, and as traffic moves ahead and the roadway surface changes such as the freeway nears a curve or rises or lowers into a kind of driving valley, it is likely I will now only be able to see maybe 5 car lengths ahead and say 8 car lengths behind me. Plus, even on a flat surface, other cars and trucks can block my view. The point being that the chessboard is continually expanding and contracting, doing so during the driving journey, moment to moment.

It is within that playing space that the other cars and vehicles nearby are the other chess pieces.

I am trying to align and motivate those other chess pieces to play the game in the way that I want them to do so. They won't necessarily want to play the game the way that I want to do so. I might be trying to get ahead of the car to my left so that I can get into that person's lane, they meanwhile might be accelerating and not wanting to let me get ahead of them. They could be doing so on purpose or it could be by happenstance as they are either not paying attention to my car or they have some other maneuver they are trying to execute and for which it happens to counter my move.

Normal chess is a two-player game. In the case of driving chess, presumably every driver that I encounter on my freeway commute is playing a chess game. They are each playing their own chess game, of which, my chess game intersects with them at some point in time. There are maybe hundreds of simultaneous chess games occurring as I drive to work and find myself among hundreds of other cars and their drivers during the journey.

Consider the complexity involved in this virtual kind of chess.

Hundreds of other chess players, all seeking to "win" at their chess game (let's assume a win consists of getting to their desired location as soon as possible and balanced by the safety factors of driving). Their chessboards are dynamically changing, doing so from moment to moment, just as mine is too, widening and shortening while driving along. I will eventually intersect with those other chess players when we get near to each other. Our chess play might intersect only briefly, maybe I zoom past another driver and soon have gotten far beyond their view, or it might be elongated such as when the traffic becomes bumper-to-bumper and for twenty minutes we are all stuck together in snarled traffic.

A means to reduce the complexity of perceiving this as a chess match of me against hundreds of other chess players involves making the game into a matter of it being them versus me. This metaphorical chess game is now reduced to a two-player game.

There is a morass of other players that I'll assume are in essence one overall macroscopic player, which you can think of as Adam Smith's "The Wealth of Nations" notion that they are all controlled by an invisible hand. Each of them is doing their own driving, obviously, and I am not suggesting that there is a conspiracy theory and nor that they are all fake acting aka "The Truman Show" or mind-controlled or something similar. I am merely reducing the perceived complexity by making this into a more traditional two-player setting. I represent me, and all of the other drivers are represented as one gigantic macro-player that involves perhaps hundreds of other chess players.

When you play normal chess, you are likely to get involved in trying to psyche out the other chess player.

I mention this aspect because some non-chess players assume that chess is entirely a game played without any emotion and it is simply all intellect. If you watch even the grandmasters play, you can see that before they get to a chess match, they have often tried to psyche out the other grandmaster, doing so by making remarks about the other player. During the chess match, they will at times try to psyche out the other player, giving them the evil eye or acting as though they don't have a care in the world or making a sigh at a move, etc. There are rules that prevent chess players in formal competition matches from going too far in this aspect of psyching out each other.

For some fun in terms of psyching out other chess players, you might want to one day go to watch the informal chess matches that occur in New York City at Washington Square Park or any similar venue. These matches sometimes involve "semi-pro" chess players that sit there all day long trying to make money at perhaps a few dollars per match as a wager. The ones that sit there all day are often prone to wild kinds of psyche-out approaches during a chess match. They tell you that you are smart and going to win, they on the next move tell you that you've blundered (regardless if you have), they ask you about the weather (a distraction), they warn you to be on the watch for an angry dog prowling the park (preoccupy your mind), and so on.

The point being that chess is not solely a game of disembodied beings that make chess playing choices dryly and without emotion. Human chess players are humans. This means they have all of the everyday foibles and emotions that seem to go along with being a human being. Sure, some of the chess players try for years and years to overcome their naturally occurring emotions and strictly play the game by-the-book. Some say that the Soviet Union during the Cold War tried to achieve this with their top chess players. In the end, it is nearly impossible to completely submerge and remove the emotionally charged elements from a human player.

The cars that are nearby me on the freeway are being driven by human beings. This means that they too are riddled with emotion. They will not necessarily make car driving choices that are entirely predictable by a purely rational calculation. This makes the metaphorical chess game more challenging. I cannot necessarily assume that the car driver to my left will "do the right thing" and let me into their lane. The other driver might purposely cut me off because they don't like the look of my car or maybe they don't like how I have been driving.

Besides the dangers of getting into a car accident while playing the metaphorical chess driving game, you also need to be watchful of getting into a road rage incident. If you drive in a manner that another driver dislikes, it can spark them into a kind of rage. They are going to potentially take out that rage by trying to drive their car to come after you. Whatever larger driving goal they might have had, such as getting to the grocery store, can be laid aside as they become fixated on trying to block your car or threaten you or whatever.

While doing the metaphorical driving game, there are times at which the move you might have wanted to make will be blocked or cut-off. This I realize perhaps seems obvious. We all know how frustrating it can be when you are for example trying to get off the freeway, but no other cars are letting you get into the exit lane. You curse them as you see that you've now missed your exit. They would likely have little sympathy and emphasize that you should have started toward your exit sooner. And so, the daily grind of driving and at times lack of driving civility comes to the fore.

There are also driving moments wherein you are forced into making a driving move that you didn't want to do. In normal chess, being forced into making a move that you prefer not to make is known as a zugzwang.

For driving chess, let's imagine an instance of zugzwang. You are in the fast lane and zipping along. You are eager to get to your destination and the approach so far has been to stay in the fast lane as much as possible. The other lanes of traffic are somewhat snarled, while the fast lane is moving at a really good clip. You suddenly come upon a car that is moving very slowly in the fast lane. The dolt! Don't they realize they are in the fast lane.

You come right up to the bumper of the slow-moving car. The car stays where it is and does not speed-up. You flash your headlights at the car. No response. You honk your horn. No response. This slow-moving driver seems to be entrenched in the fast lane. If you could somehow push them out of the way, you would. Your only recourse seems to be to switch lanes, this though puts you into the snarled traffic, plus you'll need to arduously make your way ahead of the slow-moving car while in the adjacent lane, and then try to enter back into the fast lane ahead of the tortoise driver. What a pain in the neck!

Do you choose to stay in the fast lane, moving now at a slowed speed, or do you make the maneuvers and contortions to try and get around the slow driver? You don't want to have to do all of those contortions since you know it might end-up backfiring and you might fall further behind in the traffic. Your preference would be to stay in the fast lane.

You've just encountered a kind of zugzwang.

This example is not a truly forced zugzwang in that you can opt to stay in the fast lane and just bear with it. There are plenty of driving examples whereby you are forced into a particular move.

The other day I was driving down a street that leads right to my desired destination, and it turns out that the police had blocked the road and were forcing all car traffic to take a detour. This was frustrating because I could see the destination and it was just a few feet on the other side of the roadblock.

Nonetheless, I had to obey the police and take the detour (I suppose I could have tried to ram the roadblock, which might have been exciting, though not legal and I'd be probably in jail right now).

While driving on a driving journey, you are likely to have an overall driving strategy that guides your overarching driving efforts. This driving strategy might be that you want to get to your destination and avoid having to drive in the bad parts of town, along with the notion that you are willing to drive more slowly than usual because you want to enjoy the scenery along the way. Your driving tactics involve the moment to moment driving moves, and they are guided by the other driving strategy that you have. Executing a right turn up ahead is a driving tactic, while the aspect of making that right turn due to the goal of getting to your destination and avoiding the bad parts of town (which say that if you proceeded straight, you'd go into), encompassed the driving strategies you've devised.

Avid chess players typically have an overall chess playing strategy and couple it with various moment to moment chess playing tactics. You might have as an overarching chess playing strategy that you like to take over the center of the chessboard. Your opponent might not be as keen on that as a playing strategy and might instead believe in going to the opponent's area and dominating that space. For each of those players, the moment they make any specific chess move, it could be that it is aiding their overall chess strategy. Not each tactical move necessarily does so, and it all depends upon the evolving state of play during a particular chess match.

Furthermore, you might adjust your chess playing strategies depending upon the nature of your opponent. For some chess players, they like to always play using the same chess strategies and for which they believe that it will beat any opponent. Other chess players might believe that you need to deploy a chess strategy that will be best suited against a particular player. I might abandon my normal default of wanting to control the center of the chessboard if I know that my opponent welcomes that kind of strategy and has come up with ways to undermine it.

There are some famous chess matches in which a top-level grandmaster suddenly switched from their traditional chess strategy and caused a stir. The opponent would likely be thrown for a loop because they had studied and prepared for the assumed chess strategy that was going to be most likely utilized. This kind of trickery can be handy, if you can pull it off well. If you switch strategies and are not as strong at the new strategy, maybe though you will do worse than if you had stayed with your tried-and-true.

Just as each chess match in normal chess is a new game, each time that you get onto the road you are starting a new metaphorical chess match.

You will have some kind of driving strategies and overarching goal, and this will be a guide during the moment to moment tactical aspects of your driving. When driving to work, you might adopt one particular set of driving strategies and tactics. Meanwhile, while on vacation in Hawaii, you might adopt a different set of driving strategies and tactics.

There are some human car drivers that seem to always have the same driving strategies and tactics. They do not particularly veer from it. This lack of flexibility will often get them into a traffic quagmire. They either do not realize that getting bogged down in the quagmire is due to their staid strategy and tactics, or they might realize it but decide to just proceed anyway, or they might be desirous of switching to a different strategy and set of tactics but do not know how, or have waited too long to do so on a timely basis that would make a difference.

I hope that my discussion about chess playing as a driving metaphor does not alarm you. There are some people that are perturbed when I bring up this topic.

Part of the basis for their being perturbed is that they think I am perhaps mocking the seriousness of driving.

By trying to apply the rules or sense of playing chess, they believe that I am not taking driving as seriously as I should. It is not a game, they would say. People's lives are at stake. There is a concern on their part that I am willing to maybe do things while driving because I am pretending it is a game, for which I otherwise would not undertake if I put aside a game-like mentality.

I assure you that I do take driving very seriously.

I am not applying a chess playing metaphor as though I am playing a video game and do not care about whether I hit other cars or strike pedestrians. My chess metaphor does not overwhelm my sense of sensibility. I can be and am a conscientious driver that abides by the driving laws and rules.

In fact, I would suggest or claim that the use of the chess metaphor actually aids and informs your driving ability. The more that you think about how to best drive, it would seem hopefully the better the driver you become. It seems to me that drivers that put little thought into their driving are more likely to be the ones that end-up causing accidents or creating untoward traffic situations. They are caught unawares because they are not putting sufficient cognitive cycles toward the driving task.

This brings up a related question that I sometimes get about the chess metaphorical driving. If my mind is used up by thinking about chess aspects of driving, wouldn't this imply that I am perhaps over-thinking driving? Maybe I am putting too much thought into the driving process. There are some that believe you either know how to drive or you do not. By over-thinking it, you are presumably going to be a worse driver. You are using up precious and limited cognitive cycles that should instead be devoted to just driving, and not thinking about driving.

I counter-argue that the notion that more knowledge about something makes you worse at it, well, it's an old line that I don't think typically bears out. Is my mind so preoccupied with trying to figure out driving tactics and my driving strategy that I become oblivious to the roadway situation and therefore will tend toward getting into a car accident? I would assert that is the actual anti-thesis of the point of the chess playing metaphor, which is to do a better job at driving, including calculating the amount of cognitive effort going towards the driving task and being responsive to the real-time demands of the driving matters at-hand.

Anyway, I certainly hope that my discussion doesn't alarm you. In addition, don't try to become mentally engaged in considering your driving as a chess match if it will indeed cause you to become preoccupied or distracted from the act of safe driving. Whatever means you have of driving a car, if it seems to be working, probably best if you continue with it.

I bring up the chess playing metaphor not to somehow convince other humans to do so, but due to the notion that we can examine and understand to some degree the driving task via the use of a chess metaphor. Out of which, it might help us to devise AI and automation to tackle and undertake the human driving task, as you'll see in a moment.

AI Self-Driving Cars and Chess Play

What does this have to do with AI self-driving cars?

At the Cybernetic AI Self-Driving Car Institute, we are developing AI software for self-driving cars. The use of chess as a metaphorical way of looking at driving can be quite insightful, and aids in the advances being made towards developing true AI self-driving cars.

Allow me to elaborate.

111

I'd like to first clarify and introduce the notion that there are varying levels of AI self-driving cars. The topmost level is considered Level 5. A Level 5 self-driving car is one that is being driven by the AI and there is no human driver involved. For the design of Level 5 self-driving cars, the auto makers are even removing the gas pedal, brake pedal, and steering wheel, since those are contraptions used by human drivers. The Level 5 self-driving car is not being driven by a human and nor is there an expectation that a human driver will be present in the self-driving car. It's all on the shoulders of the AI to drive the car.

For self-driving cars less than a Level 5, there must be a human driver present in the car. The human driver is currently considered the responsible party for the acts of the car. The AI and the human driver are co-sharing the driving task. In spite of this co-sharing, the human is supposed to remain fully immersed into the driving task and be ready at all times to perform the driving task. I've repeatedly warned about the dangers of this co-sharing arrangement and predicted it will produce many untoward results.

Let's focus herein on the true Level 5 self-driving car. Much of the comments apply to the less than Level 5 self-driving cars too, but the fully autonomous AI self-driving car will receive the most attention in this discussion.

Here's the usual steps involved in the AI driving task:

- Sensor data collection and interpretation
- Sensor fusion
- Virtual world model updating
- AI action planning
- Car controls command issuance

Another key aspect of AI self-driving cars is that they will be driving on our roadways in the midst of human driven cars too. There are some pundits of AI self-driving cars that continually refer to a utopian world in which there are only AI self-driving cars on the public roads. Currently there are about 250+ million conventional cars in the United

States alone, and those cars are not going to magically disappear or become true Level 5 AI self-driving cars overnight.

Indeed, the use of human driven cars will last for many years, likely many decades, and the advent of AI self-driving cars will occur while there are still human driven cars on the roads. This is a crucial point since this means that the AI of self-driving cars needs to be able to contend with not just other AI self-driving cars, but also contend with human driven cars. It is easy to envision a simplistic and rather unrealistic world in which all AI self-driving cars are politely interacting with each other and being civil about roadway interactions. That's not what is going to be happening for the foreseeable future. AI self-driving cars and human driven cars will need to be able to cope with each other.

Returning to the topic of chess, let's consider how the playing of chess relate to the advances being made toward developing true AI self-driving cars.

Chess Playing AI in Modern Times

I'll start my discussion with a quick overview of the progression of game playing by citing AlphaGo Zero to AlphaZero, which are well-known game playing AI-based programs, and also discuss Deep Blue, an AI-based chess playing game that defeated the world chess champion in 1997.

If you are interested in the underlying details about those game playing applications, you might want to take a look at the December 7, 2018 issue of Science magazine that has an article entitled "A General Reinforcement Learning Algorithm that Masters Chess, Shogi, and Go Through Self-Play" and has a handy link to pseudocode depicting some of the algorithms involved.

IBM's Deep Blue (or some called it Deeper Blue) application achieved popular notoriety when in May 1997 it was able to best Garry Kasparov, the reigning world chess champion at the time, doing so in a final score of 3 ½ games to 2 ½ games (a draw was worth a half point) and the chess match abided by the official chess competition rules including time constraints.

If you like conspiracy stories, here's a quick aside for you about the momentous occasion. There was some controversy about this win by Deep Blue, namely that Garry Kasparov later accused the developers of changing the code of Deep Blue during an actual match, specifically in the second game, and thus he claims he was beat not solely by a computer but by human intervention that adjusted the code to try and beat him.

The developers indicated that they did not change the code during the game play, though they did say that they changed the code between each of the games, which apparently was allowed by the rules of the chess match. One could say that the code changes between games would be somewhat equivalent to a human chess player that between games might confer with other notable chess experts and adjust their game play for the next games of the match, based on the advice given by those other chess experts.

Anyway, back to the crux of things that the nature of Deep Blue was that it had been based on the data of thousands upon thousands of positions and chess games, out of which an evaluation function was mathematically formulated. The evaluation function would take as input the chessboard pieces and positions and spit out what the next move should be. The evaluation function was subdivided into specialties. There were around 8,000 different segments or portions of the evaluation function, each having a particular specialty as to the chess game status.

You might liken this to having a whole bunch of chess experts sitting next to you while playing a chess match, each having a particular expertise in terms of maybe at the opening of a chess game, or during the middlegame, or during an end game, and you would confer with the appropriate specialist at the time of the game that it made sense to do so.

In addition, the program had a database of over 4,000 opening game positions and around 700,000 grandmaster games. The application had been pieced together with the assistance of various grandmasters consulting with the developers of the code. During a chess match, the code would do a look-ahead to try and ascertain various moves and counter-moves, which is referred to in game playing as levels of ply.

Generally, the deeper that you look ahead at moves and counter-moves, the better off you will be in terms of making a good move right now. If one chess player looks only at say one or two moves ahead, they might not realize that at move number three or four they are going to get trounced. Meanwhile, if the other chess player can imagine ahead to a level of three or four moves, they might be better off and know what they can do to trounce the player that only looked ahead one to two levels. Novice chess players often are only able to "see ahead" perhaps one to two ply, while grandmasters can presumably envision many ply ahead.

Deep Blue was setup to consider at times six ply to eight play ahead, and in other cases look ahead at 20 ply or more. I'm guessing that some of you might be wondering why you would not always look ahead as far as possible, maybe looking ahead to the very end of the game. In essence, when at any given state or position of the chess game, why not try to imagine all of the moves and counter-moves that would lead to the end of the game and therefore you could anticipate whether the move you might make now will lead to you winning, losing, or earning a draw.

This brings up a point I had been making earlier about time.

If you had unlimited time to make a choice, you could presumably try and figure out each and every move and counter-move that might arise. When people used to mail their chess moves to each other, you might have days or weeks to ponder the moves and counter-moves. During chess competitions that are timed, you only have so many minutes or seconds to make your choice, thusly you need to bound how far ahead you are imagining the game play, since the imagining aspects take up precious time.

When you consider that the game of chess has a chessboard of 64 squares and there are 16 chess pieces per player, and each chess piece moves in certain ways, the number of potential moves and counter-moves can be a quite large number. A famous mathematician named Claude Shannon calculated that the game-tree complexity of chess was around 10 to the 120th power as a conservative lower-bound (see his 1950 paper entitled "Programming a Computer for Playing Chess"). There is a chart that some use to depict this by saying that after each player in a two-player chess match has made only 5 moves each, the number of potential possible games that could arise henceforth from that position is around 69,352,859,712,417.

In short, there is both good news and bad news about trying to look ahead in a game like chess.

I'll give you the good news first. The good news is that since the game has a defined and finite number of boards positions, and a finite number of pieces to be played, plus there are rules that define legal moves versus illegal moves (you cannot make illegal moves), there is presumably a finite number of potential moves that can occur. Some estimates put this upper bound at around 10 to the 50th power or something similar. I mention this because in some games and other venues we might not have any end in sight as to the number of potential moves and therefore be fighting against trying to figure out something that essentially can never end.

The bad news is that the moves space is vast enough in chess that you are unlikely to be able to have the time to consider all the potential moves ahead. You need to therefore look ahead far enough that you can, as allowed by the time provided, and hope that by looking that far ahead you'll be making a better decision now, versus not having looked that far ahead. The moves and counter-moves are usually portrayed as a tree-like structure, branching out for each of the moves and counter-moves. You need to be mindful of the time allowed in terms of doing a search through the tree.

Speaking of time, moving forward in time to today's game playing applications, AlphaGo Zero and Alpha Zero have departed from the Deep Blue kind of coding that was dominant during the 1990s and into the early 2000s. The older method was to create an elaborate evaluation function, which I've mentioned Deep Blue had, and do so via a smorgasbord of handcrafted human provided tweaks and twists. The search space for the tree search was relatively large and not especially confined, and the algorithm used to do the tree search was the alpha-beta search approach.

The alpha-beta tree search uses two key factors, called alpha and called beta, which are used during the search through the tree that represents the various moves and counter-moves ahead in the game. Alpha is used to represent the minimum score that the player seeking to maximize their score will get depending upon which move they might make, while beta is the maximum score that the other minimaxing player would get. In a simplified manner, if you walk through the moves and counter-moves on a pretend basis, I would want to maximize my chances of winning while you would want to minimize my chances of winning. Therefore, at each move, I try to pick the maximum winning choice, and you would counter with picking the minimum winning choice for me.

This is a popular way to walk through a search space and it is known as the minimax approach. Alpha-beta augments the minimax approach by including a pruning feature. Essentially, the pruning involves opting to no longer pursue a particular path of the tree if it is considered unlikely to offer any viable advantages. This is helpful because it can cut out swaths of the tree.

It would be as though you are standing in your backyard looking at a massive tree and trying to decide how to climb to the top of it. You might have many branches that you can try. Upon closer inspection, suppose you realize that there are branches that seem unlikely to reach the top or otherwise are not advantageous to use, and thus you "prune" those branches and no longer give them consideration. This will reduce your effort of trying to determine which branches are worthy of closer attention.

The use of alpha-beta tree search and the evaluation function was considered state-of-the-art as to an AI-based set of techniques to use for game playing, and what made it feasible for Deep Blue was the use of parallel computing to help out. An RS/6000 computer with 30 nodes and with 480 chess-devoted VLSI processor chips was used to run the program. The code was primarily written in C and the OS was AIX. This was considered a supercomputer at the time and could assess around 200 million positions per second.

Today's AlphaGo Zero and the newer AlphaZero have shifted away from the use of an elaborated evaluation function that was coupled with the use of the alpha-beta tree pruning algorithm. Instead, the latest approach consists of using a Deep Learning reinforcement algorithm based on Artificial Neural Networks (ANN), and coupling this with the use of the Monte Carlo Tree Search (MCTS).

In brief, it is a large-scale neural network that is considered "deep" because it has a multitude of layers and many "neurons," and it uses "reinforcement learning" in the sense that it does self-play and rewards itself or penalizes itself based on what happens during the self-play (that's called reinforcement), leading to it being able to adjust the neural network accordingly for future play.

The Monte Carlo Tree Search involves once again creating a tree of the moves and counter-moves, but it does so on an expanding basis, meaning that it tries to avoid having to construct an entire search space and only construct the portion that has promise. The "Monte Carlo" part of it has to do with selecting a random sample of the search space, in a sense it is making a gamble about which part of the subtrees to explore (just as though you have gone gambling at a casino in Monte Carlo!).

Why is the Monte Carlo Tree Search attractive over the use of the alpha-beta pruning algorithm or similar kinds of approaches? Here's why it is handy for game playing like chess:

- Does not need nor use an explicit evaluation function (so, no more handcrafting, as was required in the case of Deep Blue, and avoids the human-laden aspects of getting the application up-to-speed).

- Monte Carlo Tree Search does not need what is referred to as a "developed theory" about how to play the game being considered and instead applies generally to game playing of most kinds (thus, this can be applied to chess and other games such as Go, Shogi, etc.).

- You can halt the MCTS at any juncture of its effort, while it is assessing the next moves, and you will still have a viable result that can be used (versus with other techniques you need to let them run until they fully complete otherwise you have nothing particularly useful in-hand about what to do next).

- The search time by MCTS should be lessened than that of alpha-beta pruning because of the short-cuts used, though this is not to say that MCTS will be "perfect" and so you are also taking a risk or willingness to have it prune something that might turn out to be significant.

What's interesting too about AlphaZero is that it uses the neural network to figure out on its own the proper settings of itself, based on perhaps hundreds of thousands of self-played games, rather than having a human handcrafting the code. This included that the approach was able to "discover" aspects such as opening moves that seem good to use, versus if it had been fed thousands of already prescreened opening moves that were hand selected for it to use.

I think this is sufficient to cover the essentials of today's chess game playing approaches versus those of yesteryear.

Though the newer approaches are impressive, I don't want you to infer that they are more capable than they really are. I've seen some pundits gushing with enthusiasm that say that the AI-based techniques now "understand" how to play chess. Hogwash. If you are suggesting that these techniques are the equivalent of human "understanding" then you've got to be able to also explain to us how humans understand how to play chess. As I've mentioned previously, no one knows as yet.

I would say that hopefully we are on a solid path towards improving how we develop AI systems and that those AI systems will continue to be improved in their performance. Chess provides a handy laboratory, as it were, within which we can tryout different AI approaches and push the boundaries of what AI consists of.

The Driving Task and Chess AI Techniques

I've laid the foundation of the nature of today's chess playing AI techniques and I'd now like to explain how this dovetails into the arena of AI self-driving cars.

We'll begin with the sensors of AI self-driving cars. There are a myriad of sensors such as cameras for capturing images and video, there are radar sensors, ultrasonic sensors, LIDAR sensors, and so on. The data collected by those sensors needs to be assessed and interpreted. Based on the assessment and interpretation, the AI system will then be able to figure out what needs to be done next in terms of driving the car.

Does an image that was just captured contain a car in it? Is the car near to the AI self-driving car or far ahead of it? Is there a pedestrian in that image? Is the pedestrian near or far away? Somehow, the sensor detection and interpretation aspects of the AI self-driving car need to discern what kinds of objects are out there surrounding the AI self-driving car.

This sensory input and interpretation are happening each and every moment that the AI self-driving car is underway. It needs to be undertaken in real-time. If the detection and interpretation take too long, the AI might not have altered the course to avoid hitting say another car that has suddenly come to a halt in front of the AI self-driving cars. The sensory data interpretation also needs to be done with a great deal of accuracy in the sense that if the detection and interpretation fails to identify a car ahead or a pedestrian standing there in the street, it could be a life-or-death consequence.

By what AI-based technique or approach can we use to be able to do this kind of detection and interpretation of the sensory data? Furthermore, it needs to be fast so that it works in the real-time constraint confronting a self-driving car. It also needs to be relatively reliable and accurate, otherwise there is going to be untoward results.

There is no magic that will make this happen. We need to use whatever AI techniques or approaches that can be identified and will work best for this need.

To-date, much of this interpretation is done via the use of Artificial Neural Networks (ANN). A neural network is trained beforehand to identify objects in say images or radar data or whatever, such as finding cars, light posts, pedestrians, and the like. This trained neural network than is loaded on-board of the processors in the AI self-driving car and takes as input the raw sensory data, perhaps being transformed somewhat by other routines first, and then tries to identify the objects in the data.

Having the ANN "learn" during the act of the AI driving the car is rather chancy right now, since it could be that the neural network mistakenly learns something that is real-world untoward and then misleads the AI system by duping it. Instead, the ANN is typically prepared beforehand and pushed as a kind of executable into the on-board systems. Data collected from the sensors might be uploaded via OTA (Over The Air) electronic communications to the cloud of the auto maker or tech firm, and further ANN refinements might be undertaken at the cloud level, and then pushed down as patches or updates into the on-board ANNs.

When you consider chess playing such as the use of Deep Learning with reinforcement, coupled with the Monte Carlo Tree Search, we can use the same AI techniques for doing the sensory data assessment and training for the deep ANNs for an AI self-driving car. This can be done in the backroom, so to speak, when preparing the ANNs for use on-board the self-driving car.

There is also the possibility of doing so in real-time while the AI self-driving car is underway, depending upon the boundaries that we put around the scope of the learning and also the speed at which it can perform. This is ongoing research.

I want to clarify that when I've presented this at conferences, there are some that initially think I'm referring to the idea that the chess playing system might be say using a camera that is pointed at the chessboard and doing image capture of the chessboard and where the chess pieces are. Nope. That's too easy. I'm referring to the chess playing Deep Reinforcement Learning (DRL) going on related to the chess moves and chess playing.

Which takes us to the next aspect of an AI self-driving car, namely the sensor fusion. During the sensor fusion, there is an attempt to bring together the various sensors and their interpretations and reach conclusions or at least estimations of what objects are being detected via the sensors. Once again, we can use the DRL and MCTS to help with this aspect.

The AI self-driving car then updates the virtual world model which indicates the status of the objects surrounding the self-driving car. It also has attributes about those objects such as whether they are in motion or stationary, where they are most likely headed, their speed and projected speed, etc.

This then takes us to the heart of the AI self-driving car, or some might say the "brain" in that the AI action planning is where the crucial analyses occur about the status of the self-driving car and what the next actions will be.

Note that I put the word "brain" in quotes because it is not at all like a human brain and I don't want anyone to infer from my use of the word that I am somehow implying it so.

Remember earlier herein when I took you through my chess playing metaphor for the driving of a car?

Well, this is where we can especially make use of the chess playing AI techniques, now that we are discussing herein the stage of the self-driving car processes that involves trying to ascertain what driving moves to make. Similar to my mental model of perceiving my car as in the middle of a chessboard and that each driving action was a kind of chess move, so too we can consider the AI self-driving car to be doing likewise.

The AI action planning portion of the self-driving car needs to incorporate the latest status of the surroundings as exhibited via the virtual world model. The virtual world model is kind of like a souped-up chessboard that indicates the pieces of the driving surroundings and what their status is. The AI has to take a look at the present state, and using the driving strategies and driving tactics, derive the actions that need to be taken next. The AI will then issue driving command controls to the self-driving car accordingly.

This is of course happening in real-time. Just as in chess there is a time constraint, likewise there is a time constraint for the AI of the self-driving car. It cannot try to explore all possible ways in which to next move the self-driving car. As mentioned earlier, the real-time constraints in driving are more severe than chess playing, both in the amount of time allowed to make a decision and also the consequences of making a wrong or bad decision.

In my example earlier of my trying to get ahead on the freeway, I considered the cars immediately near me and those just a few ahead and behind me. Had I also looked further up ahead and behind me, I might have had many more cars to consider in terms of my possible moves and their possible counter-moves. I essentially trimmed my mental search space by confining my move calculations to those cars directly near me (was I using alpha-beta in my head or was I using MCTS, don't know, you tell me!).

Rather than being a chess playing metaphor in the mind of a human driver, we can embody the same kinds of principles into the AI self-driving car system and particularly in the AI action planning element.

Consider these aspects about my daily drive to work:

- Chess strategy => Driving Strategy = overall approach to driving the self-driving car, style of driving, overall journey goal, etc.

- Chess tactics => Driving Tactics = moment-to-moment driving actions such as switching lanes, taking an exit ramp, allowing another car into my lane, etc.

- Opening game => Driving Journey Start = backing out of the garage, driving down the local street, making way to the freeway

- Middlegame => Driving Journey = getting onto the freeway, navigating and maneuvering while on the freeway, getting off the freeway, etc.

- Endgame => Driving Journey End = nearing my office, local streets, driving into the parking lot, finding a parking spot, parking.

Some of today's AI action planners take a rather simpleton approach to driving the self-driving car.

For example, they look only for lane markers to determine where the self-driving car should be positioned, and then do a follow-the-leader kind of driving involving following whatever car is directly ahead of the self-driving car. I refer to this as the pied piper approach.

Those simpleton approaches are not going to get us to a true Level 5 AI self-driving car. They are only stopgaps on the way to getting there. If we stay with just those rudimentary approaches, there is little hope of achieving a true AI self-driving car.

In that sense, just as we have progressed from the AI techniques used in the 1990s that served us well then for aspects such as Deep Blue winning at chess over a grandmaster, today we have advanced toward the DRL and MCTS along with faster hardware, all of which allows even greater levels of play and at preferably faster speeds.

The same kind of incremental advances are going to be evolving as AI self-driving cars are improved in terms of the autonomous driving capabilities. AI techniques will be pushed forward by the desire to achieve true AI self-driving cars. The advent of AI self-driving cars will be pushed forward by improvements in AI techniques and processing power. There is a synergy between AI and the aspects of AI self-driving cars as a kind of application of AI.

I've also pointed out the synergy between chess and AI, in which AI pushes forward and we can see it take place via chess as an application, and likewise the playing of chess advances because of those advances that perchance happen in AI.

I'm an advocate of finding the synergy between all three, namely chess, AI, and self-driving cars. That's the kind of moves needed to get AI self-driving cars to become real competition with human driven cars. As an old Chinese proverb says, life is like a game of chess, changing with each move. We need to keep changing up the AI for reaching the vaunted goal of true AI self-driving cars. That move makes sense.

CHAPTER 6

COBOTS EXOSKELETONS
AND
AI SELF-DRIVING CAR

Lance B. Eliot

CHAPTER 6

COBOTS EXOSKELETONS
AND
AI SELF-DRIVING CAR

I remember the first time that I saw a cobot in action. It was on a factory floor where I had previously helped put in place a robotic arm that performed automotive parts assembly. This cobot, considered a collaborative robot or a co-robot, or some assert it should be referred to as a "cooperative" robot, contained some of the latest new tech in AI.

First, let me tell you about the "aged" robotic arm that I had put in place a few years earlier. It was enclosed in an overall steel-mesh cage that served to prevent humans from getting too close to the swinging mechanical arm. With the speed and strength of the robotic arm, a human caught unawares and within the range of the arm would surely get injured. There was little to almost no sensory capability on the robotic arm for detecting any intrusions into its operating space. This somewhat low-tech "dumb" robotic arm was able to swing back-and-forth unimpeded to do its job.

In the case of the cobot, it was designed and built to be near to humans and work in unison with humans. I had done some of the underlying research in my university lab when I was a professor that involved several projects pioneering cobot early development.

Now, I had been invited to see a cobot in action on a factory floor, doing so within earshot of the old-timer robotic arm that I had programmed some years prior.

The cobot had no protective cage surrounding it. Indeed, there was a workstation just a few feet from the cobot that housed a human worker. The human worker would do part of an assembly and then hand over the partially done part to the cobot. The cobot then did its effort of furthering the assembly. Once the cobot had finished, it then slid the part back to the human worker. The human worker made a few finishing touches and then placed the part onto a conveyer belt that would take it to the installation phase of the manufacturing process.

There were some AI developers that were hoping to ultimately replace the human worker by further refining the cobot, allowing the cobot to do the entire effort of the assembly for the part. At this time, the intricate aspects of the assembly required a great deal of dexterity. The cobot was mainly an arm with pincher-like grippers and lacked any fully articulating robotic fingers. It was up to the human to use their own human hands and human fingers for the fine task of weaving wiring throughout the part.

This splitting of the task made good sense in that the robotic arm could quickly undertake its effort and was able to do so as a "partner" with the human. If the cobot could have done all of its work and completed the part assembly sufficiently that the part could move forward to the installation phase, you probably would not have needed the human and cobot to work in unison. Instead, because the cobot was essentially in the middle of the assembly, taking a partial assembly from the human, and handing back a further partially assembled part, the intermixing of the human and cobot made sense.

To avoid having the human in-the-loop, it would be necessary to either get a cobot that had greater dexterity with human-like robotic fingers or consider redesigning the part so that it could be assembled differently. The AI developers had studied the existing assembly process that had previously involved humans doing the entire three steps, the pre-wiring, the assembly, and the post-wiring, and had decided that since they were told that the redesign of the part was not going to occur, they would then craft a cobot to take on the step 2 in the process.

I earlier mentioned that there was a workstation adjacent to the cobot that housed the human assembler operator. In actuality there were four such workstations in a star-like pattern that were situated around the cobot. The cobot would do its thing for one human operator, and then swing to the next human operator to take their partially assembled part, and so on, doing this for each human in a successive sequence.

Let's number the humans as operators H1, H2, H3, and H4.

H1 does pre-wiring, the cobot grabs the part, does its thing, and slides the part back over to human H1 for the operator to do the post-wiring and then finish the assembly. The moment that the part was sliding over to H1 from the cobot, the cobot was already swinging next to human H2. The cobot would take the pre-wired part from H2, continue the assembly, and slide it back over to human H2. Swinging to human H3, the cobot would take the same actions, and then swing to human H4, after which the cobot would swing once again to human H1 and start the loop again. This was repeated over and over.

I suppose a human sitting where the cobot was anchored might get dizzy of all-day swinging around and around in a tight loop. Not the cobot. It did its thing without complaint or nausea. The four humans that sat within arm's reach were able to somewhat chat about the cobot amongst themselves (the cobot was relatively silent and did not make much noise, there was no squeaking or beeping, but the factory floor was overall quite noisy and so the humans had to speak-up to be heard over the din of the factory itself).

The cobot was not listening to the human workers per se. It did though have an audio input capability akin to Alexa or Siri. A human worker could yell out a codeword to get the attention of the cobot and then state a command, such as "stop!" or other verbal instructions. Admittedly, I did wonder if the cobot might be "listening" or even recording the scuttlebutt being spoken by the four humans surrounding the cobot. The head of the factory insisted that the cobot audio detection was only scanning for the activation codeword and otherwise was not recording anything. I'll assume this was a truthful explanation (but, if I was one of the human workers, I would be skeptical!).

If a human worker was late in handing over their part, the cobot would skip the human and proceed to the next human worker in the sequence. Pretend that human H2 had fallen behind. When the cobot finished the effort underway with human H1, it would swing to H2, but if H2 did not readily handover the part, the cobot would swing to human H3. At that juncture, the human H3 might not yet be ready, since the person wasn't expecting the cobot at that moment. The cobot would wait for the human H3 to be ready.

The cobot had been programmed to keep track of the number of times that any of the human workers in its star were late in doing their respective assembly. This lateness metric was then provided to a human supervisor. If the human supervisor noticed that a human worker was falling behind excessively, the human supervisor would come over to talk with the human worker to find out what was going on.

In that sense, the human workers of the star, humans H1, H2, H3, H4 considered the cobot to be a bit of a tattletale. I suppose that if the cobot could really talk, it would tell the humans H1, H2, H3, and H4 that there was nothing it could do to prevent itself from being a tattletale. It had been programmed to do so. What do you want it to do, lie to the boss?

Anyway, the humans in a star were working steadily and did not have much time to do any idle banter or messing around. The movement of the cobot served to also be a reminder of the timing involved in getting your human work done. As soon as the cobot returned your part to you, you knew that you had to finish the pre-wiring, put the part onto the conveyor belt, get the next part, do the pre-wiring, and be ready by the time the cobot had swung around in sequence and ended-up back at your workstation.

I noticed that the human workers would keep their eye on the cobot. At first, I thought that might be due to concerns about getting whacked by the cobot.

Allow me to explain.

My years earlier robotic arm was safely nestled inside a steel cage, unlike the cobot. The only chance of hurting a human with the aged robotic arm would be that a human would need to open the door to the steel cage and go into the area reserved for the robotic arm. This would be stupid to do. In fact, it would be nearly impossible to get yourself hit by the robotic arm because the moment you opened the cage door, I had programmed the robotic arm to come to a halt. This was a prudent safety precaution.

For the cobot, the four humans arrayed in a star around the cobot were all and each completely vulnerable to potentially getting hit by the cobot. Suppose that the cobot "lost its mind" and went wild, swinging itself around and waving its arm crazily. Those four humans would likely get hit. The speed of the cobot was so fast that I doubted that any of the humans would have been able to duck or retreat prior to getting hit. The only way I could envision avoiding getting hit would be if the cobot made some preliminary indication that it was going berserk, in which case the humans might have sufficient time to hide or run away.

To prevent the cobot from going into a human-damaging berserk mode, the AI developers had put sensors onto the cobot that were intended to detect the chance of hitting a human. If you put your human arm up and placed it into the path of the cobot, the cobot would detect the intrusion and would stop itself from moving in that direction. It would also emit a prerecorded message telling the nearby humans that there was an intrusion in the path of the cobot.

I tried this to see how well-programmed the cobot was. I sat at a workstation and jammed my arm into the path where the cobot would soon be traveling. Sure enough, it detected my arm and did the proper stoppage procedure. I wondered whether I could "trick" the cobot by swinging my arm into the path at the last possible moment, tempting fate by not allowing enough time possibly for the cobot to make the detection and then come to a halt.

Since I didn't want to potentially lose my actual arm, I used a stick instead. I raised up the stick with a last split second to go before the cobot arm would have reached my workstation. I was relieved to see that the cobot detected the stick and once again exercised the proper stoppage operation. The stopping time was quite quick and the detection capability seemed robust. Generally, I deduced that the safety feature was likely good enough that it would be some oddball quirk before a human could get hurt.

When I say that it could be a quirk, we don't know how well the cobot had been exhaustively tested. Maybe there were some unknown or hidden loopholes in the detection or the stopping procedure. Maybe there are some bugs in it. Who knows? Knowing that you are sitting eight hours a day within the grasp of a gorilla that could tear off your limbs, this for me would be somewhat disconcerting.

The human workers though had seemingly become comfortable with the cobot. The only reason they were staring at it was that they knew the troubles they would get into if they weren't ready when the cobot showed-up at their workstation.

For Amy, sitting at workstation H1, she knew that once the cobot had reached Eric at workstation H3, it was time for her to have placed the part onto the conveyor belt and already be starting the pre-wiring of the next part that was intended for her effort. Had Amy seen that the cobot was at Judith on workstation H4, it would suggest that Amy was going to be late in having her part ready when the cobot got finished at H4.

It was almost as though the human workers hoped they could mentally convey to the cobot to slow down when they needed it to let them catch-up.

A human sitting in the cobot's position could perhaps be negotiated or pleaded with. Hey, give me a break, will you, and nudge down just a fraction of a moment to let me take a breath and be ready for when you swing over to me. There was no such negotiation or discussion with the cobot.

After "visiting" with the cobot and observing it in action, along with watching the human workers and discussing the cobot with them, I next went into a conference room that was attached to the factory floor. There the R&D group showed me a prototype of a cobot exoskeleton.

In case you've not seen a cobot exoskeleton, imagine that you are wearing a kind of suit of armor, but it is in a skeleton or skeletal kind of shape. Some refer to these as exoframes or exosuits.

There are "dumb" exoskeletons that exist today for allowing humans to lift heavy weights. You put on the exoskeleton. You get comfortable with how it operates. You can then grab a heavy box to be lifted. The exoskeleton takes the brunt of the weight and the lifting. You can repeatedly lift heavy objects and by-and-large the exoskeleton is taking the strain and pressure.

In some cases, the exoskeleton is purely mechanical and unpowered. In other cases, the exoskeletion is powered and it is electrical or battery power that enables it to especially do the heavy lifting or take on similar kinds of tasks. You can use the exoskeleton for more than just heavy lifting of objects. Suppose you are having to hammer a nail that is on the ceiling and it is going to take a long time to hammer that nail.

Your arms reaching over your head will eventually seem to get heavy and it will be hard for you to keep your arms raised. With an exoskeleton, you could likely keep your arms raised all day long and not feel much pain or angst in doing so.

A cobot exoskeleton is considered a "smart" version of an exoskeleton. The notion is to add AI to the exoskeleton and turn it into a collaborative robot that you wear. The cobot that I had seen on the factory floor was pretty much anchored into a specific spot on the floor. It was not moving and was not intended to be portable. Suppose instead that a human wore a cobot, allowing the human and the cobot to potentially move around. Ergo, a cobot exoskeleton.

For the aged robotic arm that I had setup for the factory, some of the arm's instructions had been programmed, while other aspects of the arm's efforts were undertaken by a Machine Learning (ML) approach. We had moved the robotic arm to show it what we wanted it to do, and after repeated such guidance it gradually "programmed" to how we wanted it to perform. Some cobots have a similar capability of using deep learning or Machine Learning. An advanced cobot exoskeleton would likewise have such a ML feature.

What does this have to do with AI self-driving cars?

At the Cybernetic AI Self-Driving Car Institute, we are developing AI software for self-driving cars. One interesting exploratory project involves the use of a cobot exoskeleton for purposes of aiding a human in the driving of a car. I realize this seems a rather farfetched approach to driving, and I agree it seems an unlikely path toward the autonomous or semi-autonomous driving of cars, but I figured you'd be intrigued by the idea and want to know about it.

Allow me to elaborate.

I'd like to first clarify and introduce the notion that there are varying levels of AI self-driving cars. The topmost level is considered Level 5. A Level 5 self-driving car is one that is being driven by the AI and there is no human driver involved. For the design of Level 5 self-driving cars, the auto makers are even removing the gas pedal, brake pedal, and steering wheel, since those are contraptions used by human drivers.

The Level 5 self-driving car is not being driven by a human and nor is there an expectation that a human driver will be present in the self-driving car. It's all on the shoulders of the AI to drive the car.

For self-driving cars less than a Level 5, there must be a human driver present in the car. The human driver is currently considered the responsible party for the acts of the car. The AI and the human driver are co-sharing the driving task. In spite of this co-sharing, the human is supposed to remain fully immersed into the driving task and be ready at all times to perform the driving task. I've repeatedly warned about the dangers of this co-sharing arrangement and predicted it will produce many untoward results.

Let's focus herein on the true Level 5 self-driving car. Much of the comments apply to the less than Level 5 self-driving cars too, but the fully autonomous AI self-driving car will receive the most attention in this discussion.

Here's the usual steps involved in the AI driving task:
- Sensor data collection and interpretation
- Sensor fusion
- Virtual world model updating
- AI action planning
- Car controls command issuance

Another key aspect of AI self-driving cars is that they will be driving on our roadways in the midst of human driven cars too. There are some pundits of AI self-driving cars that continually refer to a utopian world in which there are only AI self-driving cars on the public roads. Currently there are about 250+ million conventional cars in the United States alone, and those cars are not going to magically disappear or become true Level 5 AI self-driving cars overnight.

Indeed, the use of human driven cars will last for many years, likely many decades, and the advent of AI self-driving cars will occur while there are still human driven cars on the roads.

This is a crucial point since this means that the AI of self-driving cars needs to be able to contend with not just other AI self-driving cars, but also contend with human driven cars. It is easy to envision a simplistic and rather unrealistic world in which all AI self-driving cars are politely interacting with each other and being civil about roadway interactions.

That's not what is going to be happening for the foreseeable future. AI self-driving cars and human driven cars will need to be able to cope with each other.

Returning to the topic of cobots and exoskeletons, let's consider some aspects about the driving of a car and the use of automation to do so.

One approach to driving a car involves building all of the automation into the car itself, including the sensors to detect the surroundings, and the computer processors to run the AI software that does the driving, and so on. I'll call this the "AI-integrated" approach.

We might decide that rather than trying to integrate the automation into the car, perhaps we might instead build a robot that can get into and out of the car, akin to a human being, and the robot will be imbued with the ability to drive a car. I'll call this the "AI-robotic" approach.

For those of you that have never considered the idea of having a robot drive a car, it is worthwhile to take a moment and ponder the matter. Imagine that if you could build such a robot, it could then drive presumably any of the millions of today's conventional cars. There would be no need to change the design of cars. There would be no need to retrofit existing cars. A car would be a car.

The driving robot would be a robot. When the driving robot gets into the car and sits behind the wheel, you have a completely "backward compatible" approach to automating the driving of cars. Since the robot is sitting there at the wheel of the car, we'd hope and assume that it can fully drive the car. By this I mean to suggest that the robot can't be only partially proficient in driving a car. It might be fully equivalent to a human driver.

I realize that you could argue that perhaps we might split some of the difference, namely juice up the car so that it has some amount of automation to be able to drive, and then have a robot that also has some of the ability to drive. The car alone cannot drive itself. The robot alone cannot drive a conventional car. Instead, you might come up with a semi-automated car that can be driven by a semi-automated robot. Sure, I suppose that's a possibility.

You might even suggest that this walking-talking kind of robot might not be fully capable to drive a car and yet have other handy uses anyway. Maybe it can help humans into and out of the car. Maybe it can do chores around your house like cleaning the house and cooking meals. Meanwhile, it can also be somewhat of a chauffeur, but only if the car itself also has some of the proficiency that perhaps we cannot otherwise build into the robot.

For example, the robot might not be equipped with sensory devices like LIDAR, radar, ultrasonic, etc. Those sensory devices could be bulky and cause the robot design to get overly large and cumbersome. Thus, the robot needs to have those capabilities built into the car that it drives.

Once the robot gets into the car, it is able to plug into the AI system of the car and become "at one" with the car. This symbiotic aspect makes us achieve a one-plus-one equals two kind of merger. Each helps the other. When the robot is finished driving, it unplugs itself from the car and gets out of the car, moving along to do whatever other chores or tasks it can do.

There's another approach that also goes beyond today's usual thinking, namely the use of a cobot and an exoskeleton. In this use case, a human that wants to drive a car gets into a cobot exoskeleton first, and then steps into the car and sits at the steering wheel.

The human contributes certain aspects of the driving effort, while the cobot exoskeleton does other aspects. In one such scenario, the car is a conventional car and all of the driving task is borne by the human wearing the cobot exoskeleton. Another scenario involves splitting the driving task among the human wearing the cobot exoskeleton and having some form of semi-autonomous features built into the car.

We then have these three overall approaches involved:

- AI-Integrated Driving: All of the automation built into the autonomous self-driving car

- AI-Robotic Driving: All of the automation for driving is built into a robot, the car can be a conventional car or have semi-autonomous features

- AI-Human Cobot Exoskeleton Driving: Human and a Cobot work together to drive a car, the car can be a conventional car or have semi-autonomous features

In this latter case, the human is considered in-the-loop of the driving.

I realize that for purists, the notion of keeping the human in-the-loop would seem to undermine the overarching goal of having self-driving cars or at least fully autonomous driving (note that the AI-Robotic driving is not strictly speaking a self-driving car, instead it is a car that is autonomously driven by a robot).

As a short aside, some use the phrase robot car, or the phrase of robo-car and robo-taxi, when referring to a self-driving car. I don't like using those wordings because they confound the idea of a robot driving a car with the notion of the AI-integrated approach wherein the car drives itself.

I realize you might suggest that there's a "robot" hidden inside the self-driving car and therefore want to call it a robot or a robo-car, but I think that's an unfortunate confounding. For me, if there really is a robot that is going to step into the driver's seat, I'm Okay with saying it is a robo-car or robot car or robo-taxi, otherwise, if the AI-integrated approach is being used then I vote for calling it a self-driving car.

Having gotten that terminology conundrum off my chest, let's get back to the aspect that there are likely self-driving car purists that might have a hefty bit of heartburn about potentially keeping a human in-the-loop of driving a car.

There are several potential reasons why keeping a human in-the-loop might make sense.

First, suppose that after trying and trying to remove the human from the loop of driving a car, AI development and advancements are unable to achieve a truly autonomously driven car. No matter what tricks or techniques are devised and employed, imagine that it just is not feasible to arrive at either a self-driving car of a Level 5 or that there is no means to construct a robot to do so either. What then?

I would suggest we would want to then find a means to keep the human in-the-loop. It could be that we only need the human for edge cases or corner cases of the driving task. This might be dicey in that I've already offered many reasons why co-sharing the driving task with humans and automation can be problematic. In any case, the odds are that inexorably we are going to as a society be aiming to increase the autonomous nature of cars and so having a human involved, if that's the only way to get there, so be it, I suppose.

Another reason to potentially keep the human in-the-loop of driving might be due to humans insisting that the want to remain in-the-loop.

There are self-driving car pundits that say we must eliminate all human driving on our public roadways if we are going to reach the vaunted life-saving goals of having self-driving cars. Besides my earlier point that you cannot just magically sweep under the rug the millions of existing conventional cars, and I've also countered and essentially debunked the claim that we might merely alter our roadway infrastructure to have a two-tiered infrastructure, one for self-driving cars and one for human driven cars, we must also consider the societal question of whether humans will readily and willingly give up their driving privilege.

I know that the pundits would say that certainly people will gladly handover their driver's licenses if they knew that by doing so they would save lives. I'd say that's quite a leap in logic and faith in how people think and are motivated. I realize another angle is that people won't want to drive once they get accustomed to the grand convenience of being self-driven. Again, I have my doubts that everyone will see things that way.

I suppose it could be that after asking for people to voluntarily stop driving themselves, and to then deal with those that won't capitulate willingly, there could be a law that makes it illegal for humans to drive. Those holdouts for human driving would then be caught and penalized. Maybe if the culture shifts and we gradually as a society no longer view driving as a kind of "right" and begin to see things differently that you might be able to regulate legally this last remaining "you'll remove the steering wheel from my dead cold hands" segment of society. All of this seems a very long ways off in the future.

Meanwhile, back to the matter at hand. Let's assume that for whatever reason you like that there are those that will want to be human drivers or that we might need human drivers to make the "last mile" toward nearly full automation.

In that case, perhaps the AI-Human cobot exoskeleton might be helpful. This blends together the human driving capability with the cobot driving capability and as augmented by the exoskeleton.

The exoskeleton might aid your use of the driving controls. The arms of the exoskeleton augment your arms when using the steering wheel. The legs of the exoskeleton augment your legs when working the brake pedal and the accelerator pedal. The cobot might be controlling the exoskeleton arms and legs, and guiding your arms and legs as appropriate during the driving task.

There you are, sitting in the driver's seat, wearing your cobot exoskeleton. While driving on the freeway, a car in another lane starts to veer into your lane. Maybe you failed to notice the veering car, but fortunately the cobot did, which then guides your arms to turn the steering wheel to avoid the veering car, along with pushing further on the accelerator pedal to get away from the intruding car. Saved by the cobot exoskeleton driving AI system.

Suppose you go to the company Friday night party and have a bit too much to drink.

You get into your car to drive home.

You are wearing the cobot exoskeleton when you get into the car (no need to have been wearing it at the company party, unless you are trying to make some kind of fashion statement!).

Even though you probably should not be behind the wheel of a car, the cobot exoskeleton ends up doing most of the driving and gets you home in one piece.

You might have some kind of physical disabilities that would normally inhibit your ability to drive a car, and yet the cobot exoskeletion could allow you to drive a car.

You might need some cognitive added help when driving a car, and the cobot exoskeletion can do so.

Perhaps novice teenage drivers might be required to initially wear a cobot exoskeletion suit to aid in learning how to drive a car. And so on.

Conclusion

For many people, the aspect that we might have self-driving cars is already a kind of science fiction story that appears to be coming true. Furthermore, and separately, Cobots on our factory floors make sense. Exoskeletons make sense too, and especially for working in situations involving the physical brute capability that an exoskeleton can provide. We've all seen various science fiction depictions of exoskeletons for especially future military applications, such as shown in the movies *The Matrix* and in *Edge of Tomorrow*.

Does it make sense to consider having cobot exoskeletons?

And if so, would it further make sense to have ones that can help humans drive a car?

Seems like a rather radical notion.

Right now, the path appears to be the emergence of the AI-Integrated self-driving car first and foremost, and then maybe the longshot would be an AI-Robotic self-driving car, if we otherwise cannot achieve the AI-Integrated approach. The melding of a human driver and a cobot exoskeleton suit to do driving does not appear to be on any near-term horizon per se, but I don't think we can reject it entirely and just dismiss it fully out-of-hand.

For the time being, I'd vote that we keep our eyes open to possibilities that might seem outrageous right now, since we might need to find alternatives or want alternatives further down-the-road.

I'm thinking about making a cobot exoskeletion that could allow me to drive like a NASCAR driver, and if so, don't be surprised when you see me at the winner's circle of the Indy 500. That will be me waving, along with my cobot exoskeleton driver's suit.

CHAPTER 7

ECONOMIC COMMODITY

AND

AI SELF-DRIVING CARS

CHAPTER 7

ECONOMIC COMMODITY

AND

AI SELF-DRIVING CARS

Will AI self-driving cars be an economic commodity?

That's the scuttlebutt these days that some are predicting. There seems to be a rumor circulating which asserts that once we actually achieve true AI self-driving cars, it will be a commoditized business. I've had both industry outsiders and insiders ask me about this matter, doing so at the conferences I've been speaking at, and even at local events and collegial dinners. The rumor appears to be gaining speed.

I'd like to tackle the argument that precipitated that kind of assertion.

Bottom-line: I don't buy into the commoditization logic and nor rhetoric.

In my view, those that seem to be fostering such an indication are regrettably somewhat misguided in their logic and have perhaps fallen into some logic-traps that would hasten their belief in the notion. There are others that are going along with the notion since it sounds alluring and the surface-level rationale appears to be viable at a quick glance. My herein assessment at a deeper level suggests that the commoditized-camp and its converts might want to reconsider their stance.

Of course, we don't any of us know for sure what the future will bear out, but I'd be willing to wager that AI self-driving cars are not likely to become commodities.

First, let's start the discussion by considering what an economic commodity is. We need to all somewhat agree on the definition of an economic commodity so that we can then try to figure out whether true AI self-driving cars will become one. If we cannot agree to a definition, we'll be arguing past each other and never see eye-to-eye.

Generally, an economic commodity is considered any economic good or service for which there is an abundance of fungibility, which means that instances of the good or service are essentially indistinguishable from each other and buyers do not perceive any material distinctions about the good or service. Notice that I've mentioned that it can be either a good or service, though by-and-large it is usually a good or product that gets into the commoditization category rather than a service.

Why not services, you might ask? When offering a service, there is frequently a greater likelihood that the service being offered is differentiated, including how and who offers it, and thus they will be distinguishable in the minds of buyers.

I might need a plumber to come over to my house to deal with my leaking faucet. The Ace Plumbers service provides so-called smell-good plumbers that will show-up on-time and do a good job for a reasonable price. The Zany Plumbers service has plumbers that are typically late to arrive, they often fail to fix the plumbing problem, and they are dirty and gruff to deal with and charge an arm and a leg to do the plumbing work. It is relatively apparent that we could distinguish these plumbing service providers from each other, therefore we might say that the plumbing service is not commoditized.

In terms of goods, I'm sure that you likely know that often times products such as gasoline, sugar, grains, are referred to as commodities. They are called commodities because presumably the buyers of those products do not see any material factors that differentiates them (by this I mean that gasoline is not differentiated from other gasolines, sugar is not differentiated from other sugars, etc.). These commodities are often sold in bulk to those in the supply chain that will ultimately get them to the consumer. This tends to squeeze out profit margins because there is no particular factor that makes any better or worse than the other.

Given that they are otherwise considered equals, the providers of those commodities are fully at the whim of the marketplace in terms of pricing and they cannot try to adjust their price higher based on their product per se. If I'm selling a thousand gallons of gasoline in bulk, and someone else is selling a thousand gallons of gasoline in bulk, and if there is no differentiation between our gasoline product, it then comes down to price. I cannot try to have a higher price in this circumstance since the buyer of the bulk gasoline would be unwise to buy from me at a higher price when they can get the same thing from someone with a lower price.

Dealing in commodities can be a rough business. Dog eat dog, so to speak. I am reminded of the famous line by Karl Marx, in which he stated: "From the taste of wheat, it is not possible to tell who produced it, a Russian serf, a French peasant or an English capitalist" (for this quote and other economic theories, see the famous book "Capital: The Process of Circulation of Capital," published in 1885 by Fridrich Engels and with Karl Marx's notes, which provides the core elements of Karl Marx's economic theories).

In short, commodities are indistinguishable in the minds of buyers. This implies that the product or service can be offered by multiple sellers and yet the buyer does not recognize any differences about the product or service being sold by those sellers.

The buyer can presumably choose any of the sellers and will be buying the same product or service. If that's the case, it becomes a war on pricing among the sellers. Whomever can sell the product or service at the lowest feasible price would garner the buyers to buy from them.

Keep in mind that there are several caveats about this notion of commoditization.

The buyer has to be savvy enough to realize that the product or service is indeed a commodity. Often times, a buyer might not know this and will therefore proceed to pay a higher price for something that in theory they have overpaid on price.

The faucet in my house is running wildly and water is flowing out everywhere. Yikes, I'm in a panic. I need to get a plumber pronto. I do a quick online search and up pops the Ace Plumbers and the Zany Plumbers. As far as I know, they are both equal. I can get the same plumbing services from either one. I look quickly to see which ones has a lower price. The pricing posted by Zany Plumbers is lower than the Ace Plumbers and so I contact them and arrange for them to come to my house.

Little did I realize that the Zany Plumbers are in fact differentiable from the Ace Plumbers, recall my earlier description of the two plumbing services in which I depicted that the Ace Plumbers were more professional and the Zany Plumbers much less so. The plumber that shows up from Zany Plumbers is a miserable, grumpy, ill-prepared dolt and fails to fix my faucet properly. I did not realize beforehand that the two plumbing services were not commoditized.

Thus, the buyer needs to be astute enough to know when a product or service is indeed commoditized:

- If the buyer fails to realize something is a commodity, the buyer might be fooled or lulled into paying a higher price when there is presumably no justification in doing so.

- If the buyer believes something is a commodity when in fact it is not (it is non-commoditized), the buyer might buy at a price that seems equal to the other sellers pricing, but in the end get ripped-off by having gotten a lesser product or service than they could have gotten from another seller.

In a marketplace of goods and services, it can be difficult for a buyer to know what a commodity is and what is not a commodity.

There are sellers that might try to have the buyer believe there is a commodity in that good or service, when there actually is not. The Zany Plumbers probably wants you to think that all plumbing services are the same, hoping that you will pick them, and they are either going to try to confuse you into believing that all plumbing services are the same or they anticipate you won't research well enough to know.

This reminds me of the bottled water industry. I knew a top-level executive at one of the largest bottled water firms. He told me over dinner one night that he could not believe that people think that there is any difference between the bottled water products. It is clean water in a plastic bottle. He claimed that the water is really about the same no matter which bottled water you pick. The core product, if you consider it to be the water, he expressed was really a commodity.

To try and get buyers to believe it is a non-commodity, the bottled water company shaped the bottle in a distinctive manner and slapped flashy graphics and colors onto the exterior of the bottle.

They also boldly indicated that their water had only a miniscule amount of a certain kind of iron in it, but he told me that all of the bottled waters have about the same amount. Furthermore, he indicated that the iron content really didn't matter because it wasn't a health issue and had nothing to do with any kind of difference in taste.

In that sense, they were trying to make a commodity seem like a non-commodity. Why? Because it would allow them to convince buyers into buying their product over the other sellers, and possibly also pay a higher price when doing so. If the bottled waters are really a commodity, the buyers should be looking only at price and ignore the shape of the bottle and its flashy exterior.

For those of you that are in the bottled water business, please don't write me to complain that I've suggested that the bottled water business is a commodity industry. There are a lot of businesses that the same argument can be made that the core product or service is really in a sense a commodity, and yet the sellers in that industry try to package or portray their product or service as a non-commodity, inducing buyers to believe that the products or services are not commoditized. I am not singling out bottled water and nor am I claiming that bottled water is a commodity – I hope that will calm the nerves of those of you in that industry.

Let's take the perspective of the seller for a moment.

If you can do so, as a seller of a product or service, you'd likely prefer to offer a non-commodity product or service. This would allow you to then charge perhaps more for your product or service than others, since buyers might be willing to pay more, assuming that they perceive your product or service differences as valued.

What can be even more galling is to be a seller in a non-commoditized product or service wherein the buyers don't realize that it is not a commodity. Imagine the plight of the Ace Plumbers. They know that they go to the trouble to have nice smelling plumbers that are professional. Perhaps this costs them more to arrange. They charge a higher price than say Zany Plumbers. But, buyers that don't know are fooled or lulled into assuming that Ace Plumbers and Zany Plumbers are indistinguishable in terms of the plumbing service, so buyers go to Zany Plumbers at times when they might have been better off to go to Ace Plumbers.

Suppose that Zany Plumbers pricing is the same as Ace Plumbers. This implies that the buyer is overpaying for what they could get from Ace Plumbers. Unfortunately, if buyers don't realize this, it is possible that Ace Plumbers is losing business to Zany Plumbers, and as a double whammy the Ace Plumbers has higher costs of offering their plumbing service. It's not fair! Those darned buyers ought to be more differentiating in their buying.

Here's the mess we have then about buyers and sellers:

- Buyers can be ill-informed and therefore believe a commodity is a non-commodity, or they can believe a non-commodity is a commodity.

- Sellers might be tempted to make a commodity seem like a non-commodity, or make a non-commodity seem like a commodity.

I mention these aspects about buyer and seller perceptions and psychology because it is vital for the notion of commodities. In theory, one might argue that all buyers are always all knowing, and all sellers are always all knowing, but that's not necessarily the case. In economics, there is an entire ongoing area of debate and research about the rational and irrational behavior of humans, which plays into how the real-world works in terms of the selling and buying of goods and services.

What does this have to do with AI self-driving cars?

At the Cybernetic AI Self-Driving Car Institute, we are developing AI software for self-driving cars. As mentioned earlier, there are some rumors floating around that inevitably the industry of AI self-driving cars will be a commodity.

In essence, it has been postulated that AI self-driving cars will be commoditized and so the buyers of AI self-driving cars will presumably consider any AI self-driving car to be indistinguishable from any other AI self-driving cars. There will be no brand or feature or other facet or factor that would cause the buyers of AI self-driving cars to consider one to be better than or worse than any other AI self-driving car.

Why would that matter?

If such a prediction is correct, it implies that ultimately the AI self-driving car marketplace will be solely determined by price. Buyers of AI self-driving cars will merely look at the price to ascertain which AI self-driving car to buy. This also means that the auto makers and tech firms that are selling AI self-driving cars are competing solely on price. As I mentioned before, price alone is a dog eat dog world.

Within the auto makers and tech firms, if they were in a commoditized market space, the only thing they can presumably do is try to cut their costs as low as possible, which then becomes their only means of competition. I say this under the assumption that if commoditized, they are unable to differentiate their AI self-driving cars via any other means, since by definition we're saying that there is no difference, i.e., they all have the same features and capabilities.

One would also assume that if commoditized, the price of AI self-driving cars will all end-up around the same price. There is no value to a buyer that pays a higher price for an AI self-driving car from one auto maker versus another. To sell their AI self-driving cars, an auto maker or tech firm would need to maintain a price close to the rest of the marketplace. Presumably, the marketplace will reach a point of a pricing that provides some economic incentive for the auto makers and tech firms to stay in the market, but only such that the price is kept under pressure because all the other auto makers and tech firms are vying on price too.

Before I jump into the fray and explain why the above scenario about the commoditizing of AI self-driving cars is highly unlikely, I'd like to provide some helpful and instrumental background about AI self-driving cars that is essential to this discussion.

I'd like to first clarify and introduce the notion that there are varying levels of AI self-driving cars. The topmost level is considered Level 5. A Level 5 self-driving car is one that is being driven by the AI and there is no human driver involved. For the design of Level 5 self-driving cars, the auto makers are even removing the gas pedal, brake pedal, and steering wheel, since those are contraptions used by human drivers. The Level 5 self-driving car is not being driven by a human and nor is there an expectation that a human driver will be present in the self-driving car. It's all on the shoulders of the AI to drive the car.

For self-driving cars less than a Level 5, there must be a human driver present in the car. The human driver is currently considered the responsible party for the acts of the car. The AI and the human driver are co-sharing the driving task. In spite of this co-sharing, the human is supposed to remain fully immersed into the driving task and be ready at all times to perform the driving task. I've repeatedly warned about the dangers of this co-sharing arrangement and predicted it will produce many untoward results.

Let's focus herein on the true Level 5 self-driving car. Much of the comments apply to the less than Level 5 self-driving cars too, but the fully autonomous AI self-driving car will receive the most attention in this discussion.

Here's the usual steps involved in the AI driving task:

- Sensor data collection and interpretation
- Sensor fusion
- Virtual world model updating
- AI action planning
- Car controls command issuance

Another key aspect of AI self-driving cars is that they will be driving on our roadways in the midst of human driven cars too. There are some pundits of AI self-driving cars that continually refer to a utopian world in which there are only AI self-driving cars on the public roads. Currently there are about 250+ million conventional cars in the United States alone, and those cars are not going to magically disappear or become true Level 5 AI self-driving cars overnight.

Indeed, the use of human driven cars will last for many years, likely many decades, and the advent of AI self-driving cars will occur while there are still human driven cars on the roads. This is a crucial point since this means that the AI of self-driving cars needs to be able to contend with not just other AI self-driving cars, but also contend with human driven cars.

It is easy to envision a simplistic and rather unrealistic world in which all AI self-driving cars are politely interacting with each other and being civil about roadway interactions. That's not what is going to be happening for the foreseeable future. AI self-driving cars and human driven cars will need to be able to cope with each other.

Returning to the discussion about whether or not AI self-driving cars will become a commodity, I'd now like to tackle the question head-on.

Monolith Myth

I'll start with the monolith myth.

You might be aware of Arthur C. Clarke's famous quote or law: "Any sufficiently advanced technology is indistinguishable from magic."

This quote is contained in Clarke's famous essay "Hazards of Prophecy: The Failure of Imagination" published in 1962 and included his so-called three laws, which by the way he jokingly kept to three laws since Sir Isaac Newton had three laws and it seemed that if Newton only needed three then Clarke figured he needed only three.

In any case, the reason I offer Clark's quote is that if you take the viewpoint that all AI is essentially the same, and you don't differentiate any differences between AI elements, you are apt to make the assertion that ultimately AI self-driving cars will be a commodity.

Consider toasters for a moment. I might claim that all toasters are the same. Magically, they are able to make toast for me. I don't necessarily know how it works. All I know is that a toaster makes me toast. As such, are we to assume that toasters are a commodity? Are all toasters indistinguishable from each other?

If you say that yes, toasters are a commodity, I'd like to point out that it is by some accounts a billion dollar global market with at least 20 major players and they seem to believe that they are selling a non-commodity. Pricing ranges quite a bit. Features range quite a bit.

When I tried to buy a toaster the other day, I was nearly overwhelmed with my options. Toast two pieces of bread or three? Toast bread and also hotdog buns? Old-fashioned timer or modern-day IoT (Internet of Things) that connects with your smartphone or smartwatch? Anti-jam capability or no anti-jam? Easy to clean or do you have to take apart the toaster with a screw driver just to keep it clean?

Before I tried to buy a toaster, I assumed that it was a monolith in the sense that no toaster could be distinguishable from any other toaster. All toasters must be the same, I assumed.

I believe that some of those arguing that AI self-driving cars will be a commodity market are assuming that all AI self-driving cars will be the same.

This is an easy mental trap to fall into.

If you aren't aware of what the AI is going to do for AI self-driving cars, you can readily make a false assumption that the AI will be the same for all AI self-driving cars.

If you aren't considering the fact that the AI is being developed by different auto makers and tech firms, and therefore the nature of the AI and what it does is going to be is different across those auto makers and tech firms, you might falsely think that all of the AI self-driving cars will have the same features.

Let's consider the nature of Level 5 AI self-driving cars. I am choosing those since they are the true AI self-driving cars in the sense of being presumably fully autonomous.

Anything less than a Level 5 AI self-driving car is essentially axiomatically a non-commodity. I don't think anyone can especially debate that point. I say this because at the less than Level 5, the auto makers and tech firms can choose what kinds of AI features they want to include into their AI self-driving car. This is similar to today's cars that have a variety of advanced auto driving features. One auto maker offers auto driving for the brakes, while another might not. One auto maker offers lane correction for their cruise control, another might not. And so on.

This will continue for Level 2, Level 3, and Level 4 of AI self-driving cars.

Indeed, for Level 4 self-driving cars, the auto makers and tech firms can define their own ODD (Operational Design Domains). One auto maker might indicate that their AI self-driving car works in the rain but not the snow, and so they define an ODD for that aspect. Another auto maker might indicate their AI self-driving works in the rain and the snow, so they define an ODD for that aspect.

You, the buyer of an AI self-driving car, are trying to decide which of the Level 4 AI self-driving cars to buy. One that has an ODD that includes rain but not snow, and the other that handles both rain and snow. Which do you pick?

Certainly, it is clear cut that you are differentiating the two offerings.

If you are the type of person that lives in a place that gets snow, I'd bet that you'd buy the AI self-driving car that has the ODD that includes snow driving. For someone like me that lives in Los Angeles (LA), hint we don't get snow in downtown LA, I'd probably opt to get the AI self-driving car that doesn't have the snow driving capability (under the assumption that the one being offered that cannot handle the snow is likely a lower price or that the price somehow encompasses the lack of snow driving in some manner or another).

Okay, so we need to then only concentrate on the Level 5 AI self-driving cars, since we are agreed (hopefully) that anything less than a Level 5 can be differentiated due to the aspect that the auto makers can choose to include whatever AI features they wish to include or have available to include (and furthermore that not all auto makers will have the same capabilities to include, with some having some features ready to go and others not).

Once we get to true AI self-driving cars, Level 5, will they all embody the same AI capabilities?

That's an easy answer: No.

An auto maker or tech firm can have a true Level 5 AI self-driving car that has different AI features than those of some other Level 5 AI self-driving car made by another auto maker or tech firm.

Suppose I am selling an AI self-driving car that can indeed drive you around without any human driver needed. It is a Level 5 AI self-driving car. Fully meets the SAE (Society of Automotive Engineers) definition for a Level 5.

My AI self-driving car has a robust Natural Language Processing (NLP) feature that allows the AI to interact with the occupants of the self-driving car. It not only asks where you want to go, it also carries on various conversations. It is keeping track of where you drive to and is able to anticipate what you might want to do. Would you like me to drive you to the grocery, since it is Tuesday afternoon and you usually seem to go shopping on that day and time?

Meanwhile, another auto maker or tech firm is selling an AI self-driving car, but it does not have the same nifty advanced NLP capabilities. It merely finds out where you want to go. It does not particularly interact with you. It does not keep track of where you've been going to. Please realize that it is still in all key respects a Level 5 AI self-driving car. There is no stated requirement that it must have the advanced NLP that my AI self-driving car has.

If you were going to buy a Level 5 AI self-driving car, which would you buy – the one I am selling that has the advanced NLP or the one offered by another auto maker or tech firm that does not have the advanced NLP?

I'd dare say that you are making your decision based on a differentiation among the Level 5 AI self-driving cars capabilities. If that's the case, you are buying a non-commodity.

In other words, there are going to be lots and lots of AI features involved in AI self-driving cars that are beyond those needed to achieve the baseline of a true Level 5 AI self-driving car. The auto makers and tech firms will readily be adding into their Level 5 AI self-driving cars a variety of such features, doing so to purposely differentiate their product from others in the marketplace.

In case you want to try and argue that the NLP example is maybe "inconsequential" as a differentiating feature, I'll be happy to take you on about that. I think it is nearly self-evident that we see today how much people like Alexa and Siri and that it is a differentiating feature in terms of devices that can talk versus not talk. Furthermore, those that use Alexa and Siri can readily indicate to you that one of them is superior in terms of NLP over the other.

I'd say that if all else is equal about two Level 5 AI self-driving cars other than one has the advanced NLP and one does not, there would be buyers that would value the advanced NLP. In that sense, I don't think you can make the case for the NLP being inconsequential. I'd say it is at least consequential, and will cause some buyers to differentiate between those Level 5 AI self-driving cars that have it or do not have it. I'm not saying that all buyers will think it consequential, and indeed there are bound to be some buyers that don't care about whether there is an advanced NLP or not.

If you are now leaning toward agreeing that maybe the advanced NLP might be a differentiator, but perhaps you are now wanting to argue that it is just one factor and I am hanging onto a thin thread, well, in that case, let's discuss other such differing capabilities.

Suppose we have one Level 5 AI self-driving car that has AI features that provide a smooth ride. When the road surface is detected as rough, the AI is able to maneuver the self-driving car in a manner that offers a less bumpy ride than you might otherwise have gotten. This involves the AI detecting that a rough road exists, it involves doing AI action planning to go slowly and steer the car around potholes and rough patches. Etc.

If you were faced with buying one AI self-driving car of a Level 5 versus another, and you were informed that one had the AI-enabled smooth ride feature and the other did not, would this make a difference? Maybe you don't care about having a smooth ride and so you might say it isn't important to you. I'd bet though that a lot of other people would relish the added AI feature that offers a smoother ride. This would be a differentiator.

One of the Level 5 AI self-driving cars offers 5G connectivity, another one does not. The use of 5G makes the time needed to do an OTA (Over-the-Air) connection with the cloud of the auto maker or tech firm much faster, allowing you to readily download the latest patches and updates into your AI self-driving car.

Other auto makers and tech firms aren't including 5G. Which would you want, the faster connecting self-driving car or the slower transmitting one? Again, a differentiator.

I can go on nearly endlessly with such capabilities.

Some of the features will be directly related to the driving task, such as the smooth ride AI-enabled feature. Some of the features will be indirectly related to the driving task, such as the 5G connectivity. You might argue that the advanced NLP is not strictly speaking related to the driving task per se, though it does have to do with the overall utility of the AI self-driving car. Anyway, I'm certainly willing to say that there are some AI-related features that perhaps have little to do with the driving task and yet will nonetheless provide a differentiating aspect of a Level 5 AI self-driving car from another one.

This then addresses the monolith myth.

In recap, it will not be the case that all true Level 5 AI self-driving cars will be the same. They will differ on features that are involved in the driving task, and other features that are related to the driving task but not directly so, and even other features that are tangentially related to the driving task but nonetheless likely valued by buyers of AI self-driving cars.

That's a non-commodity.

Spontaneous Features Myth

So far, I've tried to make the case for the aspect that even once we reach the vaunted Level 5 AI self-driving cars, they will be differentiable by their features, and thus it is not the case that all AI self-driving cars are the same and indifferentiable.

When I get to that point in my discussion, I sometimes will have someone stop me and offer the thought that Okay, it might be the case that there will be some differences initially, but eventually things will flatten out and all AI self-driving cars will be the same.

This is the spontaneous features myth.

Let's get back to my toaster conundrum. The first electric bread toaster is credited with being invented by Alan MacMasters in 1893. You can look it up.

Suppose we go back in time to the 1890's and early 1900s. Toasters are starting to be sold. They initially had a difficult time trying to perfect the heating elements. This meant that your toast might get overheated or burnt. In 1905, Albert Marsh came up with a new kind of heating element that was better than what existed for toasters at the time. Less chances of burning your toast!

Some toasters included Marsh's version of the heating element, other toasters did not. Was the better heating element by Marsh a differentiator between various toasters? Yes, definitely.

In 1921, Charles Strite invented a pop-up mechanism that would automatically get your toast to be pushed up and it was easier for you to get your toasted bread. Was this a differentiator between various toasters? Yes, definitely.

Why am I telling you about these toaster advancements? Because this went on and on. Starting in 1893, we have had improvements in toasters over the years. It is a continual cat-and-mouse game. Some new feature is invented, and some toasters have it and some do not. At any given point in time, there will be features that some toasters have, and others do not. It is of course likely that over time some features will creep into the core aspects, such as the automatic pop-up contraption. Meanwhile, something else new will be invented.

This has been going on with toasters since 1893 -- that's nearly one hundred and thirty years long!

In terms of true Level 5 AI self-driving cars, do you really think that it will come a day when they all have the same exact features? Really?

If toasters have kept changing over the 100+ years, do you think it makes any sense to suggest that AI self-driving cars, which will be one of the most advanced forms of technology ever made by mankind, they will simply all end-up with the same features?

I don't see how any reasonable person could believe that the auto makers and tech firms will not be continually battling over coming up with new AI features for self-driving cars.

Here's something for you as an example. I've mentioned in my writing and in my speeches about the dangers of humans being able to potentially prank AI self-driving cars. This consists of tricking an AI self-driving car into doing something because you know how the AI self-driving car will react. For example, if an AI self-driving car is setup to come to a stop the moment that it detects a pedestrian stepping into the street, you can pretty much guess that some pedestrians will purposely step into the street since they know the AI will force the self-driving car to come to a halt.

Today, we as humans have to gauge whether another human is going to let us step off the curb. It is the pedestrian eyeballing the human driver. There are risks involved in this dangerous game. Maybe the human driver will stop, maybe not. In the future, with AI self-driving cars, the human pedestrian will be able to potentially trick the AI into halting, simply by the human making a motion as though they are going to step into the street, whether they really are intending to go across the street or not. Maybe they really do want to go across the street, or maybe that just find joy in tricking the AI into stopping the self-driving car.

A true Level 5 AI self-driving car does not have any stated requirements about dealing with pranking. Indeed, I'd say that most AI developers and auto makers and tech firms are not even considering what to do about pranking. They are so emmeshed in just getting to a Level 5 AI self-driving car that the pranking matter is not on their radar.

I mention the pranking because we've been working on an anti-pranking solution. This is a feature that I predict will ultimately be of value to AI self-driving cars. Right now, no one really cares about it. Once we have actual AI self-driving cars on our roads, and once people figure out how to prank those AI self-driving cars, I'd bet that there will be an uproar about what to do about it.

My point is that this is a feature that probably won't enter into the mosaic of AI self-driving cars features for a very long time. When it starts to get introduced, I'd predict that it will begin with some simple kinds of anti-pranking capabilities. Over time, they will become more robust.

The key is that it won't be as though all AI self-driving cars suddenly are outfitted with an anti-pranking feature. Furthermore, those that have such a feature might have a simple version, while other AI self-driving cars have a more complex one.

I know some that have said that with OTA, all AI self-driving cars can spontaneously all have the same features.

Magically, someone is somehow going to get all of the differing auto makers and tech firms to agree to a certain kind of feature, and get all of them to adopt it into their own proprietary AI systems of their self-driving cars, and then get them to all have it downloaded into their fleet of AI self-driving cars, doing so for all AI self-driving cars of all brands and makes and models, across the globe.

Really?

How did we go from a marketplace of firms that are fiercely competing with each and each is wanting to differentiate their product from everyone else's, and now they are suddenly all cooperating and fully agreeing to have the same exact features and to implement those features in the same exact way on the same day and time?

I can only imagine this occurring if somehow the government stepped into the AI self-driving car marketplace in a really heavy-handed way and somehow mandated this kind of all-features, all-the-same, for everyone at the same time, kind of approach. Doesn't seem very realistic to me. This would be an incredibly altering force to our economy and to a rather massive industry. Seems unlikely.

Homogeneous Cars Myth

I believe that I have now generally refuted the notion of AI self-driving cars possibly becoming a commodity, which I've tried to make the case they are a non-commodity by pointing out that they will not magically converge onto the same set of AI features and that instead there will be an ongoing and at times bruising form of competition to continually come out with new features.

Let's suppose that somehow the AI features all do converge in the sense that all AI self-driving cars have exactly the same AI features and do so at the same points in time. This is utterly unimaginable in any reasonable stretch of the imagination.

But, suppose as a thought experiment we entertain this rather farfetched notion and do so to see if we can help the commodity believers.

Would we not differentiate the AI self-driving cars on other factors beyond the AI features?

Today, the car industry markets us their cars based on the color of the car, the shape of the car, the overall look of the car, and so on. Why do people buy one kind of car over another?

Many of today's cars have pretty much the same driving capabilities.

You would be hard pressed when comparing some models of cars to make the case that the reason a buyer buys one versus the other is due to the driving capabilities. Instead, it is more like the feel of the seats, the interior upholstery, the cup holders, and other non-driving related features.

Indeed, the automotive industry spends millions upon millions of dollars to study the psyche of car buyers and then tries to design the shape and look of their cars to attract those buyers. There is nearly as much effort put into the actual driving mechanisms as there is in the look-and-feel of the car.

I would assert that an AI self-driving car is still a car. By this, I mean that people will still buy a car based what a car looks like and what the interior is like, and so on. Set aside the actual driving capabilities and focus for a moment on all of the non-driving aspects.

Some commodity believers seem to think that we are going to end-up with homogenous cars.

In this theory, all cars, and let's say that we end-up ultimately with all and only AI self-driving cars, will be the same look, the same shape, have the same interiors, etc.

Really?

If you look at the futuristic designs by many of the auto makers, you can readily see they are diverging already in terms of what the size of their future cars might be and what the interiors might be like. Why would the auto makers decide to merely copycat each other in terms of the look-and-feel of their cars? It doesn't seem to hold water. It is without any reasonable logic.

I know that there are sketches made by some futurists and animators that try to portray a world in which we all are riding in the same identical looking AI self-driving cars. I think this is the same as the idea that we will all dress alike in the future. We will all wear the same jump suit, universally available, which simplifies life. It also wipes out the fashion industry.

When I see such homogenous futuristic how-we-will-live predictions, it reminds me of the Dr. Seuss story that I used to read to my children when they were young, telling the tale of the Sneetches. Do you know the stars upon thars story? Please take a look at it. The point of my bringing it up is that even if we all were issued the same looking jump suits in some kind of strange Big Brother kind of future, I would bet that some people would want to add something to their jump suit to make it look different. It is human nature, I claim.

Are we going to end-up with AI self-driving cars that have the same identical look-and-feel, and for which from the outside they look exactly the same, and while inside they are exactly the same in terms of the layout and interior capability?

Hardly likely. I'd say straight out no.

There will be a variety of differing interiors. I've predicted, and others have too that we'll have swivel seats inside these AI self-driving cars and be able to swivel around and face our fellow passengers. Some might have seats that can become beds, allowing people to sleep while in their AI self-driving car. There will be a rich variety of ways in which the interiors will be designed and provided.

I'd argue that same is true about the exteriors of AI self-driving cars.

I know that some commodity believers would say that people won't care about the exteriors, since they will only have in mind that the self-driving car is intended to get them from point A to point B. They presumably won't care what the exterior looks like. I'm not so convinced that we are going to give up our imagery of the status of different kinds of cars, even in a world that becomes saturated with AI self-driving cars.

In any case, I doubt that you can quite make the same case about the interiors. Certainly, most would agree that the interior will become important, perhaps even more so than with today's cars. If you are going to be riding in self-driving cars, perhaps doing so a lot more than you ride in conventional cars today, I'd bet that you would care quite a bit about the interior of the self-driving car. In our shift and transformation to a mobile economy, wherein we will readily have available AI self-driving cars on a non-stop 24x7 basis, we might get finicky about the interiors.

If you are going to counter-argue that all interiors will end-up the same, I don't buy into that suggestion. In a sense, if that were true, wouldn't all interiors today be the same? They are not. People like different kinds of interiors and there is no one universally accepted only-way to arrange the interior of a car. The same will be true with the advent of AI self-driving cars.

As per my earlier points about the AI features, the interior features of AI self-driving cars will come and go, some features appearing and being clamored for by buyers, while other interior design features will tend to die out. Some interior features will be considered core, while other features will be discretionary. There will be an ongoing battle waged by the auto makers and tech firms about the nature of the interiors of their cars. Stars upon thars will rule.

The key takeaway is that we ought to not only consider the AI features as distinguishable, I'd assert that the interiors will be distinguishable, and perhaps the exteriors too (though I'm willing to concede a tad on that aspect, but not much!).

Recall that we earlier defined that a commodity is a product that is fungible and there is nothing that enables the buyer from distinguishing one such product offering from another. I claim that for true Level 5 AI self-driving cars, the AI features will be distinguishable, and furthermore the interior, and possibly too the exterior.

You will readily be able to distinguish one AI self-driving car from another. Deciding which one to buy will involve consideration of those factors.

Riding in one will also be somewhat a choice made about the factors, because I'd anticipate that people will want to ride in an AI self-driving car that best suits their needs.

I might feel safer being in the AI self-driving car that has the anti-prank features, so I purposely specify this when I request a ridesharing service to provide me with an AI self-driving car to get me to work. Or, maybe I like the AI self-driving car that has the all-bed interior and I want to use it to get me to my relatives across the country, but when I am in downtown I want the AI self-driving car that has the seats that allow me to get my work done.

That's a full suite of factors, therefore a true AI self-driving car would be a non-commodity.

No-Services Needed Myth

Let's next consider a twist that some don't consider about the future of AI self-driving cars, the services side. I'd like to share with you the "no-services needed" myth that some have about AI self-driving cars.

So far, I've focused entirely on the product side of AI self-driving cars in this discussion. It is indeed a product, just like a toaster. If you are buying a toaster, you primarily look solely at the product features. You are less likely to think about the services aspects related to the toaster. Toaster are inexpensive, and you can discard it if the thing breaks. Also, you tend to assume a toaster is going to last a long time before it breaks or falters.

For an AI self-driving car, I'd suggest that there will be a services element that can further potentially differentiate one AI self-driving car from another. In many ways, the services and the product tie together. A car is unlike a toaster. Cars are relatively expensive in comparison to a toaster. There is a lot more "moving parts" for a car and a lot more chance of things going awry with a car.

When you buy a car today, you know that inevitably you will need to do maintenance on that car. It is going to happen. You might think ahead and say to yourself, should I buy a car from auto maker X if they are known for doing a lousy job of service? Maybe you would have second thoughts about buying that car. Perhaps some other auto maker provides a car of a similar nature, but they are known for their incredible service.

I continue to have to remind some of the pundits about AI self-driving cars that a self-driving car is still a car. There are pundits that seem to live in a perfect world in which you get an AI self-driving car and it never breaks down. The car parts never wear out. How would this magically happen?

Let's be honest about cars. They have all kinds of problems. Sometimes they are a lemon from day one. Sometimes they have issues due to wear and tear. Realistically, there is maintenance needed on cars. There will be maintenance needed on AI self-driving cars. There will be recalls of AI self-driving cars. Etc. I know this is shocking to those that believe in a future in which cars never breakdown and never have any problems. It flies in the face of reality.

Suppose that I decide to start my own ridesharing service. I approach several auto makers that have their own brands of AI self-driving cars. Let's pretend the AI self-driving cars are all about the same (though I've mentioned repeatedly herein that I don't believe that will be the case).

One of those auto makers has a great maintenance program that takes care of the AI self-driving car bumper-to-bumper and they are well-known for keeping their AI self-driving cars in top shape. I'll call it the Ace Auto company. There's another auto maker, the Zany Auto company, known for doing a lousy job of maintaining their AI self-driving cars. Their AI self-driving cars are often in the auto shop getting fixed up.

I might say to myself, well, both of their AI self-driving cars are about the same, from a product perspective, but one of them offers a much better service in terms of maintaining the AI self-driving car. I want to keep my ridesharing fleet of AI self-driving cars going as non-stop as possible, since I only make money when those AI self-driving cars are giving paying passengers a ride. I will go with the Ace Auto company.

Aha! I just made a decision based on a differentiation related to the services side of AI self-driving cars.

We now have two ways to differentiate true Level 5 AI self-driving cars, one that is based on the AI self-driving car as a product, and the other based on the AI self-driving car and its associated services aspects.

I believe this further bolsters the non-commodity assertion, namely, an AI self-driving car is not a commodity.

Conclusion

We've walked through the reasons why I'm claiming that it seems unlikely that AI self-driving cars will become a commodity. There are those rumors out there about AI self-driving cars becoming commodities and I appreciate that those having such a belief might well have their own basis or logic for making such an assertion.

I think that many of those commodity believers are unaware of the myths aspects that I've tried to delineate herein, which are:

- Monolith myth

- Spontaneous Features myth

- Homogeneous Cars myth

- No-Services Needed myth

Is there any reason to worry about whether the future of AI self-driving cars might indeed be one of becoming a commodity?

You might be tempted to wonder if this is all a tempest in a teapot. Maybe it really doesn't matter if sometime in the future we see that AI self-driving cars have become a commodity.

I believe it does matter.

If those commodity believers are to be believed today, it can dampen the existing effort toward advancing AI and its use for AI self-driving cars. There might be enterprising AI developers that become disillusioned if they think that all AI self-driving cars are going to merely converge onto the same set of features and be a blur of the same repeated things.

Why fight hard now to be innovative if the end result is going to be that nothing seems any different from the other?

I've said many times that AI is helping to inspire and advance progress on self-driving cars, and likewise that self-driving cars are helping to inspire and push forward on AI technologies and techniques. There is an important synergy between the advances in AI and the advances related to self-driving cars. The CEO of Apple had likened the effort to produce a true Level 5 AI self-driving car as a moonshot, which I agree with his sentiment. Recall that when we were trying to get to the moon, it also pushed forward advances in technology that I doubt we'd have today or that it would have taken many more years to reach fruition of those technologies (if ever discovered at all).

The push toward AI self-driving cars is providing that same kind of impetus.

By spreading the word that AI self-driving cars will ultimately be a commodity, it could regrettably (IMHO) very well cause some auto makers or tech firms to figure it isn't worth the resources and attention they've been putting toward it. In the end, if AI self-driving cars are entirely indistinguishable, presumably the only thing that will matter is price. That's not much of a motivator for anyone involved in this journey.

I earnestly do not see any reasonable path of having AI self-driving cars becoming the same as say sugar or wheat. Since I earlier opted to quote Karl Marx, let's end this discussion on his quote that capitalism "brings forth living offspring, or, at the least, lays golden eggs."

Succinctly stated, AI self-driving cars will be non-commodity of golden eggs.

CHAPTER 8
ROAD RACING
AND
AI SELF-DRIVING CARS

CHAPTER 8

ROAD RACING
AND
AI SELF-DRIVING CARS

When I was in college, a friend of mine had a "hotrod" car that he doted over and treated with loving tender care. One day, we were at a red light and another souped-up car pulled alongside of us. For a moment, I almost thought I was in a James Dean movie, which was well-before my time, I might add, but in any case, it is generally well-known here in California that James Dean died when driving his Porsche at high speeds and ran into a Ford Tudor at an intersection in Cholame, California.

My friend glanced over at the other driver and made one of those kinds of glances that says "my car is better than your car" kind of message. The other driver looked back, slowly nodded his head as though saying prove it, and the next things I knew the engines of both cars were being revved up. There I was, sitting in the front passenger seat of my friends racing-like car and apparently, I was about to become entrenched in a road race, also sometimes called a street race.

You might find of idle interest that in Los Angeles alone there are about 700 illegal and completely unsanctioned road races each year (that's based on the latest stats collected in 2017). In some cases the road race starts just as my situation in college wherein one car driver challenges another car driver on a spur of the moment basis. In today's world, the use of social media has allowed illegal road races to become much larger and semi-organized affairs. There are social media sites that you can post your intent to engage in an illegal road race and it will give a heads-up for people that want to come and watch or perhaps directly participate.

If you are under the assumption that only the drivers would be facing the chance of going to jail for breaking the law by undertaking an illegal road race, you might want to know that bystanders can also be arrested. According to the Department of Motor Vehicles (DMV) here in California, anyone that aids in a speed contest, including those that are merely viewing it, observing it, watching it, or witnessing it, they too are violated the Speed Contest law (speed contest is another name given to the illegal road races).

In California, if convicted of participating in a speed race, you can be imprisoned for up to three months, which encompasses those doing the street racing and those "aiding or abetting" a street race. Plus, you can be fined up to $1,000, have your car impounded, and have your driver's license revoked. I remember one such illegal road race here in Los Angeles that the police broke-up and arrested 109 people. That's right, over one hundred people were busted for participating, of which only a small fraction of those people was actually racing a car.

Getting back to my situation in my college days, I knew at the time that my being a passenger in a racing car would do little to prevent me from potentially being arrested, assuming that we got caught. Of the things that I might get arrested for, it did not seem like being involved in a speed contest was one of the worthy reasons (I'm not going to list what reasons would be worthy, sorry). I knew that my college buddy would consider me "a chicken" if I tried to prevent the road race from occurring.

Which was more important, the off-chance that I might get arrested for participating in an illegal road race, or being called a chicken by my friend and perhaps word spreading that I was a party pooper when it came to doing a speed contest?

Before I answer the question and tell you what I did, let's also consider some of the other reasons why participating in an illegal road race is a bad idea. The most obvious perhaps is that you can get injured or killed. It is relatively common that when a road race occurs, inevitably someone spins out of control or somehow loses control of their racing car and hits someone or something. Another racing car might get hit. Bystanders might get hit. Innocent pedestrians that had nothing to do with the road race might get hit. Other cars that had nothing to do with the road race might get hit.

In fact, one particular criticism of these illegal road races is that the drivers are often not skilled in driving a car at high-speeds and in a racing manner. These amateurs are wanna-be high-speed race drivers. They are cocky and think they can drive fast, when in reality they lack the skills and demeanor to do so properly. If they really were serious about wanting to race cars, they'd do so on a closed track in a sanctioned manner.

In proper and legal road racing on a closed track, the cars themselves are also specially prepared for sanctioned road racing purposes. These cars are outfitted with safety gear meant to protect the driver of the car. The cars might be augmented with special NOS (Nitrous Oxide System) capabilities to allow for the boosting of speed via increasing the power output of the engine. There might be special tires with extra thick tread. For the illegal road races, it is a wild west of however the racing car shows-up it might be completely done up in a flimsy manner, and there have been many instances of these cars exploding by their own means.

Another factor to keep in mind is that a sanctioned road race on a closed track is going to presumably have a proper roadway set aside for a race. The road surface is likely well prepared for a race. When the illegal road races occur, they do so wherever they can find a place to do the race. This can include quiet neighborhoods that have families and children and pets, all of which might inadvertently get dragged into or run over by the road racers. The street itself will likely get torn up by the racing cars. If the road racers lose control of their cars, they can damage property such as light poles, fences, and so on.

Sometimes the illegal road races tempt fate in additional ways. For example, a so-called Potts Race involves the racing cars trying to drive through a multitude of successive intersections and the "loser" is the first racing car that comes to a stop at a red lighted traffic signal (the phrase of "Potts" comes from the aspect that these kinds of races were quite popular in Pottstown, Pennsylvania in the 1980s). You can imagine that other cars not involved in the road racing are all at risk of either getting struck by these maniac racers or those innocent and unaware drivers might accidentally run into one of the racing cars. A recipe for disaster, either way.

To further bolster the case for not doing illegal road races, I'll mention too that often times drinking or drugs accompanies these underground events. The drivers might opt to get themselves jacked-up for the racing and the participants might do the same. Obviously, this adds to the chances that something untoward will arise. The police also point out that often there is illegal betting that takes place, and these races are ways for gangs to congregate and add to their ranks. Plus, the gangs will at times decide to after the race perform other illegal acts, and especially if they are already "lit" after drinking and taking drugs.

I'll mention another factor that I've seen many times about these illegal road races, and I'm not sure how much it also contributes to the negative aspects of road races. I'll see a bunch of similar souped-up cars all going along on the freeway or a highway, likely heading to an illegal road race. They try to stick together and thus it is apparent that they somehow are linked with each other. This would not be problematic except that they often want to do a kind of mini-race before the "real" race that they are heading to.

Thus, on the freeway or highway, they will each try to outdo each other. If there are other cars around them that are somewhat blocking their progress, they often delight in zipping around those cars. They tend to cut into and out of traffic, doing so without regard for the other drivers. They have turned the normal freeway or highway into a game for them to play, while on their way to the race. I've seen many close calls of them ramming into other cars.

In that sense, those driving to and presumably later on driving from an illegal road race are potentially menaces to the normal driving conditions. They are eager to showcase their own prowess. They want to do their own pretend car racing. I wonder how many car accidents happen due to this tomfoolery and horseplay that they do. I'd wager that besides the potential for injuries, deaths, and damages while an actual road race happens, there is some similar kind of likelihood for untoward results either just before or just after the road race occurs.

Why do these presumably licensed drivers do this? As mentioned, it can be gang related. It can also be out of boredom or having nothing else to do. It can be due to a bet or challenge to someone else. It can be as a result of a kind of pride of their own car and a desire to show-off what they have. There is a sub-culture aspect often to illegal road races, involving those that perhaps in-their-hearts love cars and racing, and maybe also like the idea of going to the edge. Some relish the lawbreaking aspects, even though they would assert that it is not much of an illegal act.

I've heard some of these illegal road racers claim that it is unfair to stop them from their efforts. They aren't hurting anyone, they'll avow. They are just having a good time. Don't the police have better things to do such as busting "real criminals" is another refrain. Given the lengthy list of dangers and downfalls of illegal road racing, I have little sympathy for such pleas. If you want to road race, do so legally and go to the right places, using the right equipment, in the right manner, would be some potential advice.

Now that I've covered some of the background about these illegal road races, let's get back to my personal dilemma while I was in college. As mentioned, I was sitting in my friend's car, and he was making a silent but clear-cut challenge to a car driver next to us, and they were both now revving their engines. An illegal road race was imminent.

Do I participate as a passive passenger, which nonetheless means I've actively been involved in an illegal act, subject to prison time and other criminal penalties due to aiding and abetting? Or, do I "chicken out" and insist to my friend that we not compete, but this will surely have him tout to the world that I backed-out and I didn't have "the guts" to do a road race.

Imagine though that we do the illegal road race and the car hits a tree, or the car rolls over and there isn't a roll cage to protect us? Or, suppose the other car crashes and they die because we played this game? Maybe we all hit other innocent cars that happen to be in the road ahead. Perhaps by dumb-luck there is a police car that catches us, and I end-up with a police record that follows me the rest of my life? All of those aspects had to be weighed against the being-a-wimp outcome.

When you are in college, these things matter, though upon reflection now it is kind of obvious to me which was the right answer.

Assuming you are on the edge of your seat waiting to find out what happened, I sheepishly admit that before I could take any action, the light turned green and the other car went ahead at a breakneck speed, tires squealing and burning rubber could be smelled. My friend, giving me a big grin, merely proceeded ahead at a normal driving pace. He had tricked the other driver. For him, he told me that it would have been a waste of his precious car's assets to race against some idiot that happened to be at an intersection during a red light with him.

Of course, that's not the only moment in my life involving the notion of road racing.

Indeed, I would suggest that we all have our own miniature moments of road racing during our daily driving. Let me share with you an example that happened just this morning.

I was at a red light and there was a lane to my left going in my same direction. A car was there. We were both at the front of the line of cars waiting for the red light to turn green. There was a lane also to my right, but it was slated to runout once you got across the intersection. You could use that lane to proceed ahead straight, though you would quickly need to merge into my lane once you passed through the intersection. By-and-large, most people used the lane that was to my right to make a right turn and did not use it to proceed ahead through the intersection.

I've always thought that this setup of the traffic structure was begging to get someone into trouble.

If there was a car in my current position and they were not looking around to realize that the lane to their right can go straight, they might inadvertently stray into that lane as they cross the intersection, perhaps cutting off a car in that lane that is trying to go straight. Likewise, a car in that lane, if not paying attention, might inadvertently panic as they go through the intersection and realize at the last moment that their lane is disappearing, and therefore attempt wildly to merge into my lane.

Well, a car in that rightmost lane pulled up beside me and it was apparent that the driver was not intending to make the right turn. In which case, I knew they would be desirous of going straight through the intersection once the light turned green. This also meant that they would quickly want to get into my lane, since their lane disappeared rapidly upon reaching the other side of the intersection.

Did this driver realize they were going to lose their lane? If so, would they be polite about it? Presumably, the driver should allow my car to proceed ahead and then they should come back behind me. In some cases, a driver in that rightmost lane opts instead to hit the gas and try to get ahead of the cars in my lane. They figure that they can race through the intersection once the light turns green, and get ahead of the other cars, allowing them to take over the merged lane and proceed ahead unimpeded.

Notice that I alluded to the notion of racing in that last statement. Yes, there was a possibility that my car would be raced by the car to my right. This would be an unsanctioned race.

Unfortunately, the roadway engineers that devised the road structure had created a circumstance that invited a kind of road race to take place. I'm sure that throughout the day, this spot has its repeated moments of miniature road races. Over and over again this would playout. Unsuspecting drivers would get dragged into a road race. It would be interesting to know how many scuffles and bumper scrapes this produced. Hopefully it wasn't leading to injuries and deaths, though it was certainly devised to encourage such untoward results.

Since I didn't know what the other driver might do, I decided I would rapidly accelerate once the green light appeared and try to get ahead of the other car. It was my hope that doing so would make it clear to the other driver that they could simply fall in behind my car. They might not realize the need to do so until after getting across the intersection, but in any case, I'd have already cleared past the intersection and so the obvious choice for that driver at that juncture would be to merely get into my lane, being positioned behind my car which had already sped ahead.

That was my plan.

When the light turned green, I sped ahead at a faster speed than I might normally do so when starting from a stopped red light to a go-ahead with a green light position. The other car in the rightmost lane though must have perhaps driven this stretch of road before, or perhaps detected the disappearing lane while sitting at the red light and therefore opted to also accelerate rapidly as a means to zip forward. The driver seemed to be intending to get ahead of me and ultimately swing into my lane, rather than a willingness to fall behind me.

The road race was on!

I looked in my rear mirror and could see that the car behind me had decided to go at my same speed and was right on my bumper. This other driver was perhaps also thinking that the rightmost lane driver should fall behind us all. Or, the driver behind me was just a pushy driver and wanted to get going fast, and maybe was oblivious to the road race situation happening. It's hard to know what the other driver behind me knew or was thinking about.

If I slowed down mid-intersection, doing so to allow the rightmost driver to pull ahead, I might risk having the car behind me ram into my car. Me and the driver behind me were both accelerating at the same pace and an unexpected braking or slow down might have caught them unawares.

Another option was to go even faster. I already had the presumed right-of-way in my lane and if I sped up it would prevent the rightmost driver from trying to get ahead of me and merge into my lane in front of me. I was sure that the driver behind me would welcome my going even faster.

At this point in time, none of us was going faster than the speed limit. I mention this because I don't want you to think that any of us were doing an outright race at top speeds. We were all accelerating at rather rapid amounts but still well-below the actual posted speed limit. As I say, this was a miniature road race.

Upon my accelerating even more, the rightmost driver did the same. Was he doing so by happenstance and merely trying to get ahead of me, or was he doing so because he felt challenged by my car and thought we were somehow immersed in a personal road race? There is always the chance of sparking a road rage by seemingly engaging someone into an even mild road race situation.

Assuming you are once again on pins and needles and wondering what happened in this miniature road race, I "prevailed" in that I got ahead of the rightmost driver and he ended-up falling in behind the car that was behind me. All in all, the situation played itself out in a matter of a few seconds. It is the kind of driving moment that most people have all the time and never give much thought to. You mentally move on.

I brought up the circumstance to try and point out that we do road racing in our daily driving. It certainly isn't the kind of road racing that brings together a hundred spectators and gets posted onto social media. Instead, our day-to-day driving challenges will at times get us into a kind of road race with other drivers, whether we pay attention to it or not.

Was this road race illegal? I suppose you could claim that it was perhaps ill-advised, and it could have led to an untoward outcome.

Maybe I should have motioned beforehand to let the rightmost driver know that I was going to give them passage into my lane and been civil about the predicament. Maybe the rightmost driver should have respected the cars in my lane and not tried to get ahead of us and waited his turn to fall in behind us. Any driving act that is considered untoward and creates a dangerous driving situation can be considered "illegal" per se, and as such I suppose you could say that we all were not showing the proper respect for the right-of-way of others and keeping safety as the top priority in our driving actions.

What does this have to do with AI self-driving cars?

At the Cybernetic AI Self-Driving Car Institute, we are developing AI software for self-driving cars. One aspect involves the AI being prepared for and able to contend with road racing.

Allow me to elaborate.

I'd like to first clarify and introduce the notion that there are varying levels of AI self-driving cars. The topmost level is considered Level 5. A Level 5 self-driving car is one that is being driven by the AI and there is no human driver involved. For the design of Level 5 self-driving cars, the auto makers are even removing the gas pedal, brake pedal, and steering wheel, since those are contraptions used by human drivers. The Level 5 self-driving car is not being driven by a human and nor is there an expectation that a human driver will be present in the self-driving car. It's all on the shoulders of the AI to drive the car.

For self-driving cars less than a Level 5, there must be a human driver present in the car. The human driver is currently considered the responsible party for the acts of the car. The AI and the human driver are co-sharing the driving task. In spite of this co-sharing, the human is supposed to remain fully immersed into the driving task and be ready at all times to perform the driving task. I've repeatedly warned about the dangers of this co-sharing arrangement and predicted it will produce many untoward results.

Let's focus herein on the true Level 5 self-driving car. Much of the comments apply to the less than Level 5 self-driving cars too, but the fully autonomous AI self-driving car will receive the most attention in this discussion.

Here's the usual steps involved in the AI driving task:

- Sensor data collection and interpretation

- Sensor fusion

- Virtual world model updating

- AI action planning

- Car controls command issuance

Another key aspect of AI self-driving cars is that they will be driving on our roadways in the midst of human driven cars too. There are some pundits of AI self-driving cars that continually refer to a utopian world in which there are only AI self-driving cars on the public roads. Currently there are about 250+ million conventional cars in the United States alone, and those cars are not going to magically disappear or become true Level 5 AI self-driving cars overnight.

Indeed, the use of human driven cars will last for many years, likely many decades, and the advent of AI self-driving cars will occur while there are still human driven cars on the roads. This is a crucial point since this means that the AI of self-driving cars needs to be able to contend with not just other AI self-driving cars, but also contend with human driven cars. It is easy to envision a simplistic and rather unrealistic world in which all AI self-driving cars are politely interacting with each other and being civil about roadway interactions. That's not what is going to be happening for the foreseeable future. AI self-driving cars and human driven cars will need to be able to cope with each other.

Returning to the topic of road racing, let's explore what an AI self-driving car should know about this topic and what kinds of actions it should be able to undertake.

First, many AI developers might argue that an AI self-driving car does not need to know anything about road racing at all. They would say that since road racing or street racing is considered illegal, and since in their perspective an AI self-driving will always and only be driving in a legal manner, there is presumably no reason or basis for the AI self-driving car to be concerned about road racing.

That's when I debunk their false belief.

Let's start by acknowledging that there are going to be instances whereby an AI self-driving car will potentially be driving in an illegal manner. Never go faster than the posted speed limit is considered by some naïve AI developers consider as an inviolable legal restriction that shall not ever be disobeyed by an AI self-driving car. Hogwash.

We all know that there are times that you will inevitably be going faster than the posted speed limit. Suppose there is an emergency and you are rushing to the hospital? If that seems overly extreme as a use case, the prevailing speed on our freeways here in Southern California is typically well above the stated speed limit (when the freeways aren't otherwise snarled) – is an AI self-driving car going to puddle along in the traffic stream and strictly be going no more than the speed limit?

So, I am arguing that simply because something is considered an illegal driving act, it is nonetheless still potentially a driving act that an AI self-driving car might need to undertake at some point in time. Therefore, the AI ought to know about it.

The act of knowing does not mean that the AI will necessarily undertake the illegal act. I say this because some of the AI developers would claim that if you give the AI system the ability to perform an illegal driving act, you are opening a pandora's box to the AI opting to routinely and wantonly perform illegal driving acts. I'll say this again, hogwash.

Knowing about something does not equate to doing it for the sake of doing it. Instead, it will be crucial that the AI be equally versed in when to perform such an act and when not to perform such an act.

Based on my remarks so far on this, at about this time I'm sure there are some AI developers that are wondering to themselves whether I am a proponent of AI self-driving cars participating in illegal road races. Am I that kind of a scofflaw that I want AI systems to encourage and abet speed contests?

No, I am not.

That being said, I think it is useful for the AI system to be wary of road racing and speed contests so that it can recognize one. Imagine that you are driving your car and you come upon a situation whereby you are able to assess the scene around you and hypothesize that a road race is brewing. As a defensive driver, I am guessing you would reason to try and get away from the area and tend to keep from getting immersed into the matter. The AI ought to be able to do the same.

Thus, it is vital that the AI be able to detect the surroundings and assess whether or not a road race is either brewing or maybe already underway. Furthermore, remember how I earlier mentioned that I saw the remnants of a potential road race by noticing cars that were going to one or that had come from one? Once again, the AI ought to be looking around for these kinds of telltale signs. It makes the AI be more defensive and drive in a manner to aim for heightened safety.

I suppose we ought to also consider another angle about the road racing topic. If we somehow restrict the AI by preventing it from ever being about to perform in a road race at all, what about sanctioned road races? Would we be preventing an AI self-driving car from participating in a closed track and legally abiding road race?

Even if you retort that it seems silly to think that anyone might want to see an AI self-driving car in a legal road race, I would hold that laughter if I were you. I'd bet that people will be eager to see AI self-driving cars race legally against human race drivers, plus they would likely enjoy seeing AI self-driving cars racing against other AI self-driving cars. Think of chess. We today have sophisticated chess playing AI systems that play against humans, and also play against other automated chess playing systems. Seems like we would have the same interest of pitting AI self-driving cars against humans and other self-driving cars.

Overall, I'd wager that we'll want to have an AI system be able to carry on a road race but have some means to inhibit it and only allow it under certain circumstances. Does this imply that we are setting ourselves up for troubles? Some might assert that if the capability exists, an enterprising owner of an AI self-driving car might hack into it to get the AI to drive in illegal road races too. Sure, it is possible, but this brings up an even larger topic, namely if an owner can hack their AI self-driving car to do illegal road racing, the odds are that the owner can hack the self-driving car to do a lot of even worse things.

In that sense, we'd better be building the AI systems for self-driving cars with sufficient security and protections that such hacks are essentially impossible to undertake. In addition, if somehow such a hack manages to succeed, we presumably might want to have the AI self-report itself or have some other means to be able to disable the hacked AI.

Here's another subtle consideration on this matter of road racing and AI self-driving cars. There are the obvious illegal road races that involve hordes of spectators and the social media underground postings. I've also though mentioned the day-to-day road races that we all encounter, such as my example of being at a red light and having a car to my right that tried to race with me across the intersection when the light went green.

That is a form of everyday road racing. What would the AI do? If the AI system was not versed in how to handle such a situation, I'd bet that human drivers would realize that they can always outgun the AI by simply racing against it.

This means that we'll have human drivers that essentially know how to "prank" an AI self-driving car. It would be akin to knowing another driver that always drives in a certain way, and so you adjust your driving style to outwit that other dimwitted driver.

I don't think that as a society we want our AI self-driving cars to be so easily bamboozled. I say this not because I somehow am worried that the AI will have hurt feelings, but instead because with the mix of human drivers and AI self-driving cars, those tricky human drivers will be trying to find an added edge over the AI self-driving cars. This can produce untoward driving behavior by the human drivers.

If I knew that another driver will always backdown and let me exit from the freeway by simply cutting in front of the driver and causing them to slow down, you'd bet that's what I'm going to start doing. If I knew that at an intersection, I could get the other driver to let me go ahead by outracing them forward, I'd likely do so all the time. In essence, human drivers will change their driving based on what they know about the inherent limitations of how the AI system is going to drive the self-driving car.

In a world in which human drivers only magically interact with AI self-driving cars, which are presumably programmed to act in the same manner all the time, it might work itself out Okay. Keep in mind though that there are other human drivers on the road too. This means that a human driver that starts to play tricks on AI self-driving cars might very well carry those tricks into how they drive against other human drivers. Meanwhile, those responding human drivers aren't going to necessarily do what the AI self-driving car does. The mishmash of AI driving styles of a restricted nature and the human wide-open styles, it will likely produce havoc on our roadways.

I know that this will encourage those pundits that will say this further provides evidence that we need to get human drivers off of the roads. I've already stated this is impractical. Some might say let's separate the human drivers from the AI self-driving cars, doing so by having special lanes or roads that are for human drivers and others that are for AI self-driving cars. Sorry, this is also impractical. The infrastructure cost and effort would be tremendous, and it just doesn't pencil out as sensible.

Via the use of Machine Learning (ML) and Deep Learning (DL), analyses of traffic and driving behavior can aid in enabling the AI to be able to contend with road racing.

Using lots of traffic and driving data, it is feasible to devise Artificial Neural Network (ANN) models to be able to gauge when a road racing situation is developing. This also needs to be coupled with the AI action plans that provide the AI with driving tactics and strategies to deal with the matter.

There is also the use of V2V (vehicle-to-vehicle) electronic communications that can help in this matter.

If one AI self-driving car detects a brewing road race that might be of merit to forewarn other nearby AI self-driving cars, the AI could let them know via a V2V message. One twist on this would be to potentially notify the authorities such as the local police or highway patrol. There is though still a great deal to be decided about how much we want AI self-driving cars to tattle on what is happening on our roadways, and a concern that perhaps we'll be going down the path of a 1984 Big Brother by the use of AI self-driving cars in this manner.

Conclusion

Should we keep the AI in-the-dark about road racing and not teach it, train it, or imbue it without any indication about road racing? Some might say we should not let the genie out of the bottle, but I would say that it is narrow thinking at-best to assume you would want the AI to be blind to the nature of road racing. I'd prefer that the AI is versed in it, being able to detect when it happens, and be able to contend with it if forced into a road racing circumstance.

I would also suggest that there will unequivocally be a need for the AI to have road racing prowess. This will help the AI to deal with day-to-day miniature road racing that happens as part of the mix of human drivers and AI self-driving cars on the roads. It would seem too that humans will relish wanting to see AI self-driving cars that can legally race, doing so in the right situations and with the proper safety precautions undertaken.

Movies like "The Fast and the Furious" have glorified illegal street racing and you can anticipate that our culture will continue to foster that kind of driving approach.

If humans are going to be fast and furious, let's make sure that the AI can be fast when needed, and of course we ought to skip the part whereby the AI becomes furious. Perhaps the movies about AI self-driving cars will be entitled "The Fast and the Faster" and we'll have eliminated the furious aspect of driving in speed contests.

APPENDIX

APPENDIX A
TEACHING WITH THIS MATERIAL

The material in this book can be readily used either as a supplemental to other content for a class, or it can also be used as a core set of textbook material for a specialized class. Classes where this material is most likely used include any classes at the college or university level that want to augment the class by offering thought provoking and educational essays about AI and self-driving cars.

In particular, here are some aspects for class use:

o   Computer Science. Studying AI, autonomous vehicles, etc.

o   Business. Exploring technology and it adoption for business.

o   Sociology. Sociological views on the adoption and advancement of technology.

Specialized classes at the undergraduate and graduate level can also make use of this material.

For each chapter, consider whether you think the chapter provides material relevant to your course topic. There is plenty of opportunity to get the students thinking about the topic and force them to decide whether they agree or disagree with the points offered and positions taken. I would also encourage you to have the students do additional research beyond the chapter material presented (I provide next some suggested assignments they can do).

RESEARCH ASSIGNMENTS ON THESE TOPICS

Your students can find background material on these topics, doing so in various business and technical publications. I list below the top ranked AI related journals. For business publications, I would suggest the usual culprits such as the Harvard Business Review, Forbes, Fortune, WSJ, and the like.

Here are some suggestions of homework or projects that you could assign to students:

a) Assignment for foundational AI research topic: Research and prepare a paper and a presentation on a specific aspect of Deep AI, Machine Learning, ANN, etc. The paper should cite at least 3 reputable sources. Compare and contrast to what has been stated in this book.

b) Assignment for the Self-Driving Car topic: Research and prepare a paper and Self-Driving Cars. Cite at least 3 reputable sources and analyze the characterizations. Compare and contrast to what has been stated in this book.

c) Assignment for a Business topic: Research and prepare a paper and a presentation on businesses and advanced technology. What is hot, and what is not? Cite at least 3 reputable sources. Compare and contrast to the depictions in this book.

d) Assignment to do a Startup: Have the students prepare a paper about how they might startup a business in this realm. They must submit a sound Business Plan for the startup. They could also be asked to present their Business Plan and so should also have a presentation deck to coincide with it.

You can certainly adjust the aforementioned assignments to fit to your particular needs and the class structure. You'll notice that I ask for 3 reputable cited sources for the paper writing based assignments. I usually steer students toward "reputable" publications, since otherwise they will cite some oddball source that has no credentials other than that they happened to write something and post it onto the Internet. You can define "reputable" in whatever way you prefer, for example some faculty think Wikipedia is not reputable while others believe it is reputable and allow students to cite it.

The reason that I usually ask for at least 3 citations is that if the student only does one or two citations they usually settle on whatever they happened to find the fastest. By requiring three citations, it usually seems to force them to look around, explore, and end-up probably finding five or more, and then whittling it down to 3 that they will actually use.

I have not specified the length of their papers, and leave that to you to tell the students what you prefer. For each of those assignments, you could end-up with a short one to two pager, or you could do a dissertation length paper. Base the length on whatever best fits for your class, and the credit amount of the assignment within the context of the other grading metrics you'll be using for the class.

I mention in the assignments that they are to do a paper and prepare a presentation. I usually try to get students to present their work. This is a good practice for what they will do in the business world. Most of the time, they will be required to prepare an analysis and present it. If you don't have the class time or inclination to have the students present, then you can of course cut out the aspect of them putting together a presentation.

If you want to point students toward highly ranked journals in AI, here's a list of the top journals as reported by *various citation counts sources* (this list changes year to year):

- o   Communications of the ACM
- o   Artificial Intelligence
- o   Cognitive Science
- o   IEEE Transactions on Pattern Analysis and Machine Intelligence
- o   Foundations and Trends in Machine Learning
- o   Journal of Memory and Language
- o   Cognitive Psychology
- o   Neural Networks
- o   IEEE Transactions on Neural Networks and Learning Systems
- o   IEEE Intelligent Systems
- o   Knowledge-based Systems

GUIDE TO USING THE CHAPTERS

For each of the chapters, I provide next some various ways to use the chapter material. You can assign the tasks as individual homework assignments, or the tasks can be used with team projects for the class. You can easily layout a series of assignments, such as indicating that the students are to do item "a" below for say Chapter 1, then "b" for the next chapter of the book, and so on.

a) What is the main point of the chapter and describe in your own words the significance of the topic,

b) Identify at least two aspects in the chapter that you agree with, and support your concurrence by providing at least one other outside researched item as support; make sure to explain your basis for disagreeing with the aspects,

c) Identify at least two aspects in the chapter that you disagree with, and support your disagreement by providing at least one other outside researched item as support; make sure to explain your basis for disagreeing with the aspects,

d) Find an aspect that was not covered in the chapter, doing so by conducting outside research, and then explain how that aspect ties into the chapter and what significance it brings to the topic,

e) Interview a specialist in industry about the topic of the chapter, collect from them their thoughts and opinions, and readdress the chapter by citing your source and how they compared and contrasted to the material,

f) Interview a relevant academic professor or researcher in a college or university about the topic of the chapter, collect from them their thoughts and opinions, and readdress the chapter by citing your source and how they compared and contrasted to the material,

g) Try to update a chapter by finding out the latest on the topic, and ascertain whether the issue or topic has now been solved or whether it is still being addressed, explain what you come up with.

The above are all ways in which you can get the students of your class involved in considering the material of a given chapter. You could mix things up by having one of those above assignments per each week, covering the chapters over the course of the semester or quarter.

As a reminder, here are the chapters of the book and you can select whichever chapters you find most valued for your particular class:

<u>Companion Book By This Author</u>

Advances in AI and Autonomous Vehicles: Cybernetic Self-Driving Cars

Practical Advances in Artificial Intelligence (AI) and Machine Learning

by

Dr. Lance B. Eliot, MBA, PhD

<u>Chapter Title</u>

This title is available via Amazon and other book sellers

Companion Book By This Author

Self-Driving Cars:
"The Mother of All AI Projects"

by Dr. Lance B. Eliot, MBA, PhD

This title is available via Amazon and other book sellers

Companion Book By This Author
*Innovation and Thought Leadership
on Self-Driving Driverless Cars*
by Dr. Lance B. Eliot, MBA, PhD

Chapter Title

This title is available via Amazon and other book sellers

Companion Book By This Author

New Advances in AI Autonomous
Driverless Cars Self-Driving Cars

by Dr. Lance B. Eliot, MBA, PhD

This title is available via Amazon and other book sellers

Companion Book By This Author
Introduction to
Driverless Self-Driving Cars
by Dr. Lance B. Eliot, MBA, PhD

Chapter Title

This title is available via Amazon and other book sellers

Companion Book By This Author

Autonomous Vehicle Driverless
Self-Driving Cars and Artificial Intelligence

by Dr. Lance B. Eliot, MBA, PhD

Chapter Title

This title is available via Amazon and other book sellers

Companion Book By This Author

Transformative Artificial Intelligence Driverless Self-Driving Cars

by Dr. Lance B. Eliot, MBA, PhD

Chapter Title

This title is available via Amazon and other book sellers

Companion Book By This Author

Disruptive Artificial Intelligence and Driverless Self-Driving Cars

by Dr. Lance B. Eliot, MBA, PhD

Chapter Title

1 Eliot Framework for AI Self-Driving Cars

2 Maneuverability and Self-Driving Cars

3 Common Sense Reasoning and Self-Driving Cars

4 Cognition Timing and Self-Driving Cars

5 Speed Limits and Self-Driving Vehicles

6 Human Back-up Drivers and Self-Driving Cars

7 Forensic Analysis Uber and Self-Driving Cars

8 Power Consumption and Self-Driving Cars

9 Road Rage and Self-Driving Cars

10 Conspiracy Theories and Self-Driving Cars

11 Fear Landscape and Self-Driving Cars

12 Pre-Mortem and Self-Driving Cars

13 Kits and Self-Driving Cars

This title is available via Amazon and other book sellers

<u>Companion Book By This Author</u>

State-of-the-Art
AI Driverless Self-Driving Cars

by Dr. Lance B. Eliot, MBA, PhD

<u>Chapter Title</u>

This title is available via Amazon and other book sellers

Companion Book By This Author

Top Trends in
AI Self-Driving Cars

by Dr. Lance B. Eliot, MBA, PhD

Chapter Title

This title is available via Amazon and other book sellers

Companion Book By This Author

**AI Innovations
and Self-Driving Cars**

by Dr. Lance B. Eliot, MBA, PhD

Chapter Title

This title is available via Amazon and other book sellers

Companion Book By This Author

Crucial Advances for AI Self-Driving Cars

by Dr. Lance B. Eliot, MBA, PhD

Chapter Title

This title is available via Amazon and other book sellers

Companion Book By This Author

Sociotechnical Insights and
AI Driverless Cars

by Dr. Lance B. Eliot, MBA, PhD

Chapter Title

This title is available via Amazon and other book sellers

Companion Book By This Author

Pioneering Advances for AI Driverless Cars

by Dr. Lance B. Eliot, MBA, PhD

Chapter Title

1   Eliot Framework for AI Self-Driving Cars

2   Boxes on Wheels and AI Self-Driving Cars

3   Clogs and AI Self-Driving Cars

4   Kids Communicating with AI Self-Driving Cars

5   Incident Awareness and AI Self-Driving Car

6   Emotion Recognition and Self-Driving Cars

7   Rear-End Collisions and AI Self-Driving Cars

8   Autonomous Nervous System and AI Self-Driving Cars

9   Height Warnings and AI Self-Driving Cars

10 Future Jobs and AI Self-Driving Cars

11 Car Wash and AI Self-Driving Cars

12 5G and AI Self-Driving Cars

13 Gen Z and AI Self-Driving Cars

This title is available via Amazon and other book sellers

<u>Companion Book By This Author</u>

Leading Edge Trends for
AI Driverless Cars

by Dr. Lance B. Eliot, MBA, PhD

<u>Chapter Title</u>

This title is available via Amazon and other book sellers

Companion Book By This Author

The Cutting Edge of
AI Autonomous Cars

by Dr. Lance B. Eliot, MBA, PhD

This title is available via Amazon and other book sellers

Companion Book By This Author

The Next Wave of
AI Self-Driving Cars

by Dr. Lance B. Eliot, MBA, PhD

Chapter Title

This title is available via Amazon and other book sellers

Companion Book By This Author

Revolutionary Innovations of
AI Self-Driving Cars

by Dr. Lance B. Eliot, MBA, PhD

Chapter Title

1   Eliot Framework for AI Self-Driving Cars

2   Exascale Supercomputer and AI Self-Driving Cars

3   Superhuman AI and AI Self-Driving Cars

4   Olfactory e-Nose Sensors and AI Self-Driving Cars

5   Perpetual Computing and AI Self-Driving Cars

6   Byzantine Generals Problem and AI Self-Driving Cars

7   Driver Traffic Guardians and AI Self-Driving Cars

8   Anti-Gridlock Laws and AI Self-Driving Cars

9   Arguing Machines and AI Self-Driving Cars

This title is available via Amazon and other book sellers

Companion Book By This Author

AI Self-Driving Cars
Breakthroughs

by Dr. Lance B. Eliot, MBA, PhD

Chapter Title

1   Eliot Framework for AI Self-Driving Cars

2   Off-Roading and AI Self-Driving Cars

3   Paralleling Vehicles and AI Self-Driving Cars

4   Dementia Drivers and AI Self-Driving Cars

5   Augmented Realty (AR) and AI Self-Driving Cars

6   Sleeping Inside an AI Self-Driving Car

7   Prevalence Detection and AI Self-Driving Cars

8   Super-Intelligent AI and AI Self-Driving Cars

9   Car Caravans and AI Self-Driving Cars

This title is available via Amazon and other book sellers

Companion Book By This Author

Trailblazing Trends for **AI Self-Driving Cars**

by Dr. Lance B. Eliot, MBA, PhD

This title is available via Amazon and other book sellers

ABOUT THE AUTHOR

Dr. Lance B. Eliot, MBA, PhD is the CEO of Techbruim, Inc. and Executive Director of the Cybernetic AI Self-Driving Car Institute, and has over twenty years of industry experience including serving as a corporate officer in a billion dollar firm and was a partner in a major executive services firm. He is also a serial entrepreneur having founded, ran, and sold several high-tech related businesses. He previously hosted the popular radio show *Technotrends* that was also available on American Airlines flights via their in-flight audio program. Author or co-author of a dozen books and over 400 articles, he has made appearances on CNN, and has been a frequent speaker at industry conferences.

A former professor at the University of Southern California (USC), he founded and led an innovative research lab on Artificial Intelligence in Business. Known as the "AI Insider" his writings on AI advances and trends has been widely read and cited. He also previously served on the faculty of the University of California Los Angeles (UCLA), and was a visiting professor at other major universities. He was elected to the International Board of the Society for Information Management (SIM), a prestigious association of over 3,000 high-tech executives worldwide.

He has performed extensive community service, including serving as Senior Science Adviser to the Vice Chair of the Congressional Committee on Science & Technology. He has served on the Board of the OC Science & Engineering Fair (OCSEF), where he is also has been a Grand Sweepstakes judge, and likewise served as a judge for the Intel International SEF (ISEF). He served as the Vice Chair of the Association for Computing Machinery (ACM) Chapter, a prestigious association of computer scientists. Dr. Eliot has been a shark tank judge for the USC Mark Stevens Center for Innovation on start-up pitch competitions, and served as a mentor for several incubators and accelerators in Silicon Valley and Silicon Beach. He served on several Boards and Committees at USC, including having served on the Marshall Alumni Association (MAA) Board in Southern California.

Dr. Eliot holds a PhD from USC, MBA, and Bachelor's in Computer Science, and earned the CDP, CCP, CSP, CDE, and CISA certifications. Born and raised in Southern California, and having traveled and lived internationally, he enjoys scuba diving, surfing, and sailing.

ADDENDUM

Trailblazing Trends for AI Self-Driving Cars

Practical Advances in Artificial Intelligence (AI) and Machine Learning

By

Dr. Lance B. Eliot, MBA, PhD

———

For supplemental materials of this book, visit:

www.ai-selfdriving-cars.guru

For special orders of this book, contact:

LBE Press Publishing

Email: LBE.Press.Publishing@gmail.com